Human Rights

BLESSINGS OF LIBERTY

HUMAN RIGHTS

BLESSINGS OF LIBERTY

Safeguarding Civil Rights

written by

William C. Lowe

Rourke Corporation, Inc.
Vero Beach, Florida 32964

Cover design: David Hundley

∞ The paper used in this book conforms to the American
National Standard for Permanence of Paper for Printed
Library Materials, Z39.48-1984.

Library of Congress Cataloging-in-Publication Data
Lowe, William Curtis, 1947-
    Blessings of liberty: safeguarding civil rights / by
William Curtis Lowe.
        p.   cm. — (Human rights)
    Includes bibliographical references and index.
    Summary: Discusses various civil rights enjoyed by
American citizens and insured by the Constitution, Bill of
Rights, and state constitutions, including the freedom of
religion, the right to due process, and equality under the
law.
    ISBN 0-86593-173-9 (alk. paper)
    1. Civil rights — United States — Juvenile literature.
    [1. Civil rights.]   I. Title.   II. Series: Human rights
(Vero Beach, Fla.)
KF4750.L69   1992   92-9756
342.73′085 — dc20   CIP
[347.30285]   AC

PRINTED IN THE UNITED STATES OF AMERICA

Contents

Human Rights

BLESSINGS OF LIBERTY

Chapter One

What
Are
Civil Rights?

Human rights are rights that are thought to belong to all people because they are human. To put it another way, human rights are principles that state how people should be treated — by other people, by organizations, and by governments. The idea that all people have rights that others should observe is an old one. The modern concept of human rights, however, appeared only about two hundred years ago, during the era of the American and French Revolutions. These revolutions introduced the modern idea of a "free nation": one whose government guarantees its citizens certain "unalienable," human rights. Today the presence or absence of human rights is often used as the standard by which a nation is judged to be free or unfree.

Though most would agree that human rights include such things as the right to maintain control over one's own life, to worship freely, and to express one's thoughts openly, the specific identification and definition of human rights are often a matter of disagreement. One way to gain an understanding of the broad concept of human rights is to divide it into different categories of rights. This book looks at those human rights that are *legally recognized*: civil rights.

Defining Civil Rights

Civil rights are those legal rights that people enjoy by virtue of their citizenship in a nation. Recognition of civil rights can be found in some of the oldest surviving laws. Hammurabi's Code, issued in Babylon in the eighteenth century B.C., for example, recognized certain rights, even for slaves. Roman law recognized individual rights, as did the English common law that developed in the Middle Ages.

In the United States, the term "civil rights" is often used to refer to those rights that are recognized by and protected by the Constitution of the United States and by the constitutions of the individual states. In Canada, civil rights are recognized in a bill of rights contained in the Canadian Constitution Act of 1982 (although the act had not been ratified by all provinces as of early 1992). Civil rights thus include constitutional rights: legal rights recognized by the same documents that created the government. While some rights, such as the right to free speech, are written directly into the Constitution, others, such as the right to privacy, have been developed through court decisions. Some rights apply to people primarily as individuals: for example, the rights that require the government to treat people accused of crimes with due process (according to procedures designed to ensure fairness). Other rights may apply to people as members of groups, such as the guarantee that all people are entitled to equal protection under the law regardless of race or religion. Some civil rights state things that government cannot do, while others allow people to call on the power of government to protect them from being mistreated by others.

Protecting individual freedom was a primary aim of the American Revolution, and the revolutionary generation was determined to safeguard the rights that had been won in the War of Independence. During the Revolution itself, specific rights were recognized and protected in the first state

The Main Exhibition Hall at the National Archives Building in Washington, D.C., houses the Constitution and the Bill of Rights. (National Archives)

constitutions, beginning with Virginia's Declaration of Rights in 1776. Civil rights were also a topic of great concern at the time that the U.S. Constitution was written. Later experience showed the need to expand and periodically update definitions of rights and liberties to include people and groups who were not considered covered by the Constitution in its original form. The growth and expansion of freedom is thus a major theme in American history.

The Bill of Rights

The legal basis for most civil rights and liberties in the United States is found in the Constitution. One of the primary goals of the people who wrote the Constitution was to create a government that would be effective without becoming so powerful that it would threaten individual liberty. In their proceedings at the Constitutional Convention (1787), the framers tried to achieve this by setting up the government in such a way that its powers would be separated: No one branch of government would be too powerful. They did not, however, try to be specific about the individual rights that should be protected.

When the Constitution went to the states for ratification, many people were concerned at the lack of a written statement protecting the individual rights that they considered most important. In order to secure approval of the Constitution, its supporters promised that once the Constitution was in effect, they would amend it to include a Bill of Rights that would guarantee a roster of specific rights.

During the first federal Congress, James Madison (then a congressman from Virginia) worked hard to ensure that the promise was kept. As a result, ten amendments were added to the Constitution in 1791. These first ten amendments have been known ever since as the Bill of Rights because they are primarily concerned with safeguarding individual rights. Many of the civil rights that Americans prize the most are to be found among these amendments.

Many judges and other authorities on the Constitution consider the First Amendment to be the source of the rights that are most important to the functioning of a free society. The First Amendment says that Congress can make no law that threatens freedom of religion. It also guarantees that there shall be freedom of speech, freedom of the press, and the freedom to meet together and ask the government to "redress" (correct) grievances.

The other amendments of the Bill of Rights also contain important rights. The Second Amendment protects the right to bear arms. Its meaning in a modern society is the subject of controversy between those who support and those who oppose gun control. The Third Amendment forbids the "quartering" (housing) of troops in private homes in time of peace; this can be done only with legal authorization in time of war. Fortunately, it has seldom been necessary to enforce this amendment.

The Bill of Rights pays particular attention to the rights of those suspected or accused of committing crimes. The Fourth Amendment provides that police officers and other officials cannot search a person's home or take a person's belongings without following certain procedures. The Fifth Amendment says that people cannot be forced to testify against themselves and may be punished only according to the "due process of law" — that is, fairly, without presuming that they are guilty until they have been tried. The Sixth Amendment reaffirms the right of an accused person to a speedy trial before a jury and allows the accused to call witnesses for the defense, and the Seventh provides for jury trials in most civil cases. The Eighth Amendment says that the government cannot require excessive bail or punish those convicted in cruel or unusual ways.

The amendments in the Bill of Rights were designed to secure the most important individual rights, but they were not intended to be the final statement on the subject. The Ninth Amendment leaves open the door to the recognition of other rights by saying that rights other than those specifically included in the Bill of Rights may be recognized. The Tenth Amendment reserves other powers — those not delegated to the federal government or denied to the states — to the states or to the people. In other words, the states may recognize rights that are not contained in the Bill of Rights.

The Fourteenth Amendment

Since the Bill of Rights became part of the primary law of the United States in 1791, special circumstances have made it necessary to add other amendments to the Constitution. Several of these later amendments provide the basis for civil rights that are considered fundamental today.

A number of later amendments deal with civil rights as they affect groups of people. Among these, none has been more important than the Fourteenth Amendment. It was added to the Constitution in 1868, during the Reconstruction period that followed the Civil War. The war abolished slavery in the United States. One of the major purposes of the Fourteenth Amendment was to safeguard the civil rights of former slaves.

Among other things, the Fourteenth Amendment provides that no state shall deny to any person the equal protection of the laws. This meant that former slaves could not be denied such basic human rights as the right to move or to make contracts. The passage of the Fourteenth Amendment marked the first time that any part of the Constitution used the word "equal" with regard to people. In the short term, the Fourteenth Amendment was not always successful in providing for the equal protection of the laws, especially in the case of former slaves and their descendants. In the twentieth century, however, the Fourteenth Amendment came to provide a constitutional basis for establishing the legal equality of all U.S. citizens, regardless of race or ethnic group.

The Fourteenth Amendment is important for another reason. The original Bill of Rights was considered to apply only to the *federal* (that is, the U.S.) government, and not to the states. In 1868, Congress was worried that some of the states might try to restrict the rights of former slaves, so it wrote the Fourteenth Amendment in language that was intended to prevent the *states* from denying former slaves (and anyone else) protection of the laws. Some of its supporters argued that the Fourteenth Amendment was written to ensure that all citizens of the United States would enjoy the rights included in the Bill of Rights: "No state shall make or enforce any law which shall abridge the privileges or immunities of citizens of the United States." This is what is called the *incorporation doctrine*: the belief that the Fourteenth Amendment "incorporates," or includes, the Bill of Rights, so that these important civil rights cannot be abused by the state governments, just as the Bill of Rights itself protects these rights from abuse by the federal government.

Much of the modern definition of civil rights has involved interpretation of the Fourteenth Amendment. At first the courts were reluctant to accept the doctrine of incorporation. Beginning in the 1920's, however, the Supreme Court and other courts began to apply most of the Bill of Rights to the states. Today, only a few of the rights listed in the Bill of Rights (ones that are less likely to be the subject of legal controversies) do not also apply to the states.

Voting Rights

Voting rights form one area of civil rights that is vital to the successful working of a democratic government. The original Constitution did not have much to say on this topic; it allowed each state to decide who could vote — and who could not vote — in that state. Here again, the Reconstruction period was important in setting an example of constitutional change.

Where To Find Civil Rights in the U.S. Constitution

Right	Amendments to the U.S. Constitution													
	1	2	3	4	5	6	7	8	9	10	14	19	24	26
Freedom of religion	✓										*			
Freedom of speech	✓										*			
Freedom of the press	✓										*			
Freedom of assembly/petition	✓										*			
Right to bear arms		✓												
No unlawful quartering			✓											
No unreasonable searches or seizures				✓							*			
Right to due process					✓						*			
Speedy trial by jury						✓					*			
Jury trial in civil cases							✓							
No excessive bail or cruel and unusual punishments								✓			*			
Recognition of unnamed rights									✓		*			
Powers reserved to states and to the people										✓	*			
Equal protection of the law											✓			
Voting rights												✓	✓	✓

*Rights that have been incorporated into the Fourteenth Amendment by Supreme Court decisions.

In 1870, the Fifteenth Amendment was added to the Constitution. This amendment said that the states cannot deny the right to vote on the basis of race, color, or the fact that a person was once a slave. Voting rights began to be extended to more people. In 1920, the Nineteenth Amendment opened the way for women in all states to vote, and in 1971 the Twenty-Sixth Amendment gave the right to eighteen-year-olds.

Do States Also Protect Civil Rights?

The Constitution may be the basis of civil rights in the United States, but every state constitution also has its own built-in protections of civil rights — often in the form of a "state bill of rights." Some of the rights listed in these state constitutions are also protected by the U.S. Constitution's Bill of Rights and the Fourteenth Amendment. Many state bills of rights are more detailed, however, and cover a larger number of rights. The right to a publicly provided education, for example, has been extended to every child in the United States, but it is a right guaranteed by the states, not by the federal Constitution. Women in some states enjoy greater constitutional protection under their state constitutions than do women in other states. Attempts to amend the U.S. Constitution to declare that equality of rights cannot be denied on the basis of sex — the proposed "Equal Rights Amendment" — failed in 1982. A number of states, however, have similar provisions in their constitutions.

Chapter Two

Why Care About Civil Rights?

Civil rights are necessary to a free society. To be free, people must be able to make choices in both their personal and their public lives. How free would people be if their governments told them that they must attend a particular church? or if it permitted only one political party? or if a person could be arrested and imprisoned simply because the police disliked that person? The answer to these questions, of course, is that they would not be very free at all.

Why Not Take Rights for Granted?

The United States, Canada, and many Western European nations generally rate highly among the nations of the world in studies that measure relative degrees of personal freedom. Individual rights and liberties are so common in these countries that the citizens of these nations hardly ever think about them. Yet many people in the world do not enjoy this extensive range of freedoms. In some parts of the world, individual rights are severely limited in the name of social order, national unity, some particular body of ideas, or even religion. A black person in South Africa is considered inferior by some whites and, according to a legal system of segregation called *apartheid*, cannot commingle with or enjoy the same rights as whites. In China's Tiananmen Square in 1989, students who were peacefully demonstrating for democracy were shot by government soldiers. In Romania, children born with minor deformities have been placed in filthy "hospitals" and treated like animals. In Iraq, Kurdish villagers have been exterminated with poison gas. These and many other people do not enjoy basic human rights, but they continue to struggle to secure these rights. Their willingness to risk their lives to be able to elect their own governments and conduct their own lives according to their own beliefs is a reminder that our fundamental civil rights are not "free": They must be fought for and constantly protected.

Americans can be, and have been, as intolerant as other peoples. Public opinion polls show that Americans overwhelmingly reply "yes" when asked if they support the Bill of Rights, but when asked about specific rights — "Should police have to have a warrant to search a suspect's house?" or "Should Communists be allowed to speak on television?" — many Americans will give answers that contradict the Bill of Rights. The answers may vary, too: If the person exercising the right to free speech is a business woman running for election to the city council, many Americans might say that she should be able to make a controversial campaign speech. Yet these same Americans might say that a homeless person standing on a park bench and shouting angrily at people during their lunch hour should be silenced.

The history of the United States provides examples of times when rights have been at risk. During World War I, for example, Congress passed the Espionage and Sedition Acts. These laws stated that those who incited resistance against the war effort, through either speech or deed, were committing an illegal act. The law was used to arrest many of those who had spoken out against the war. During World War II, many

Japanese Americans were forcibly interned in camps. Despite the fact that many were American citizens, they were thought to be disloyal simply because of their ethnic background. Civil rights have also been violated during peacetime. For many years, African Americans were denied the equal protection supposedly provided by the Fourteenth Amendment and were treated as second-class citizens. They were forced to use separate facilities in restaurants, buses, and other public places, and they were denied the same educational and employment opportunities that were open to white persons.

Perhaps the tendency not to respect the rights of those with whom we disagree or whom we dislike is part of human nature. Scholars who have studied attitudes toward civil rights have concluded that most people learn intolerance more easily than they learn tolerance. That is all the more reason that the protection of civil rights and liberties should not be left to public opinion. It is also a reason that rights should not be taken for granted. Thomas Jefferson put it this way: "Eternal vigilance is the price of liberty."

An Ongoing Process

Another reason for not taking civil rights for granted is that their meaning is constantly changing. There are many reasons for such changes.

One is that the wording of the Constitution itself is not always precise. The Fifth and Fourteenth Amendments provide guarantees of "due process" to those accused of crimes. Most would agree that *due process* means that the accused person should be treated fairly. Reasonable people may differ, however, on what exactly constitutes fairness. The meaning of the Constitution's wording has also changed over time. The Eighth Amendment forbids "excessive fines" and "cruel and unusual punishments." One hundred dollars might have been considered an excessive fine in the late eighteenth century, but today it would be thought a light fine for many offenses. Two hundred years ago, putting a person in a pillory would have been considered a reasonable punishment for some crimes; today, such a punishment would be considered both cruel and unusual.

Not only does the wording of the Constitution often need to be given more concrete meaning through interpretation; it must also be applied to conditions that could not have been imagined by its framers. The First Amendment's authors had newspapers in mind when they drew up its guarantee of freedom of the press. Today, radio and television have successfully claimed the protection of that same amendment.

Another important reason that the definition of constitutional rights is an ongoing process is that rights sometimes conflict with one another. A person accused of a crime has a right to a trial by an impartial jury, according to the Sixth Amendment, but if the case has attracted publicity, such a jury may be hard to find. Can pretrial publicity be limited without infringing freedom of the press? Which right is more important? When rights come into conflict, there is no easy answer.

Previously unrecognized rights may appear, too. The Ninth Amendment leaves the door open to the definition of such new rights. The right to privacy, increasingly recognized by the courts since the 1960's, is a good example. Just because civil rights are rooted in the printed words of a constitution does not mean that they have been fixed once and for all. The fact that their definition is a continuous process has often worked to expand our freedoms beyond the limits that existed two hundred years ago.

The Courts and Civil Rights

If civil rights are constantly being defined and redefined, a person might well ask, "Who defines our civil rights?" In the

How Civil Rights Cases Reach the Supreme Court

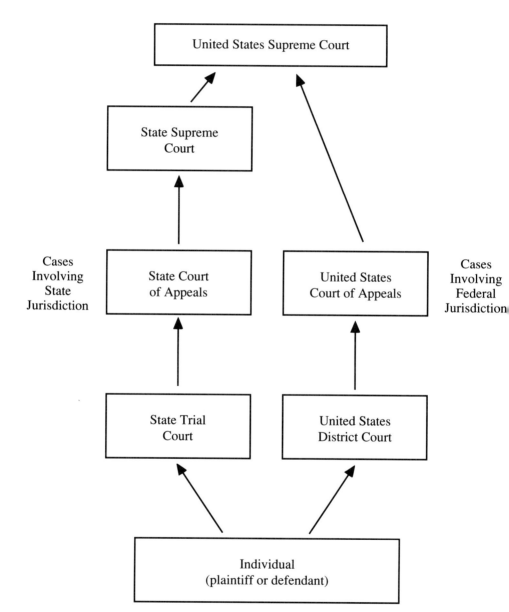

broadest sense, all citizens of a democratic society define their rights. Whenever a U.S. citizen chooses to exercise a particular right, that person is acting on the assumption that his or her action is protected by the Constitution.

In a more legalistic sense, however, the definition of civil rights and liberties is the function of the courts, especially the Supreme Court of the United States. It is the job of the courts to *apply* the law. The power of the Supreme Court to apply the nation's highest law, the Constitution, is given by the Constitution itself. Since the early days of the republic, the Supreme Court not only has applied the Constitution but also has *interpreted* it, sometimes overturning acts of Congress and state legislatures and state court decisions when it has found them to conflict with the Constitution. There is much truth to the old saying that "the Constitution means what the Supreme Court says it means." That is why people who are concerned about their civil rights spend time studying the Court's decisions.

Cases that reach the Supreme Court often require the Supreme Court justices to give meaning to a particular civil right. These cases can reach the Court in two basic ways. If the case arises under a *state* law, it will usually be tried first in a state trial court. Then it will make its way through the state judiciary system to the state's highest court of appeal. If a right claimed under the Constitution is involved, then an appeal to the Supreme Court may be filed. Cases involving *federal* law or jurisdiction will originate in the federal court system. From the federal district courts, appeals may be made to the United States Courts of Appeals (also known as "circuit courts") and from there to the Supreme Court.

The Supreme Court itself generally decides which cases it will hear, and it is very selective. In a typical year, the Supreme Court will receive between four thousand and five thousand requests to hear cases but may hear only two or three hundred. In deciding which cases to hear, the Court considers the importance of the legal and constitutional issues involved. If a case raises an important civil rights question, the chances that the Court will hear it are increased.

In deciding an appeal, the Supreme Court will usually follow earlier *precedents*; that is, it will look at earlier court decisions in related cases and apply those interpretations to the case that it is currently considering. Such cases often serve to define more clearly the meaning of a particular right. Sometimes, however, a case may raise a question not previously heard before the Court, or sometimes the Court may decide to overturn a previous decision.

A good example of the Court's overturning a previous decision occurred in 1954 in the case of *Brown v. Board of Education of Topeka, Kansas*. An earlier decision in this area of the law had stated that racially segregated schools were constitutional as long as "equal" facilities were provided. The Supreme Court reversed this decision. Chief Justice Earl Warren stated the Supreme Court's interpretation of the law as follows: ". . . in the field of public education the doctrine of 'separate but equal' has no place." When such a reversal occurs, the chances are much greater that the Court will issue a *landmark decision*, one that will determine the direction of judicial interpretations for some time to come.

Controversy over the Court's Role

The Supreme Court's power to interpret the Constitution is often controversial. Some people fear that the Supreme Court justices might try to put their own political opinions into effect, rather than adhering to the letter of the Constitution. Since Supreme Court justices are not elected by the people but instead are appointed by the President of the United States, critics of the Court often see its role as undemocratic.

Others argue, however, that someone has to interpret the Constitution, and the Constitution itself leaves the Court in the best position to do this job. They point to the Court's long tradition of avoiding questions that are considered to be primarily political. While other decisions may indeed have political effects, justices see themselves as *interpreting* the law rather than *making* the law. Making law, they have often stated, is the business of Congress.

If a Supreme Court decision is overwhelmingly unpopular with politicians and the public, it can always be overturned by amending the Constitution: Unlike acts of Congress, the Court cannot declare a constitutional amendment unconstitutional. One of the purposes of the Fourteenth Amendment, for example, was to overturn the controversial *Dred Scott* decision of 1857, which said that black people, even if free, were not citizens. Such reversals are rare, however. Most often, the Court's interpretations will stand for a long time. That is why it is so important to be aware of cases that come before the Supreme Court: The decisions that the Supreme Court makes can influence the way our civil rights are interpreted in future courts of law.

Chapter Three

Freedom
of
Religion

In the 1950's, students in many American public schools began their day in similar fashion: After reciting the pledge of allegiance to the flag, they would pray. The Lord's Prayer was popular, as were locally written prayers. The morning's prayer might also be accompanied by a student or teacher reading from the Bible.

Some students and parents in New York, however, felt that the morning routine in their local public schools amounted to enforced attendance at a religious ceremony that was financed with their tax dollars. This, they argued, violated the idea of separation of church and state, which is guaranteed by the First Amendment. They sued the local school system.

In 1962, the Supreme Court decided the case of *Engel v. Vitale* in their favor. It ruled that the requirement that students participate in prayer, even the intentionally nondenominational prayer used in New York, amounted to compulsory attendance at a worship service. Few court decisions have provoked such anger as this "school prayer decision." Newspaper headlines accused the Court of "outlawing God," and the House Judiciary Committee received a petition signed by 170,000 people, favoring an amendment to overturn the decision. A

Our society is a place of religious diversity. (Christopher R. Harris/Uniphoto)

number of amendments were proposed, but to date they have all failed. *Engel v. Vitale* is clear evidence that freedom of religion is a topic that can inspire deeply felt convictions and provoke explosive controversy.

The Establishment Clause

Two hundred years ago, James Madison and other supporters of the First Amendment believed strongly in religious freedom. Many of them had grown up in colonies where there was an "established" church: one denomination favored by law over others and supported by the taxes of all. Madison and his friends believed that this was wrong. Such an arrangement worked against the right of each individual to follow his or her own conscience in matters of religion in what was already a religiously diverse nation. Even worse, people who did not belong to the established church were required by law to pay for its support. Madison and others were determined that the United States would not have an established church.

The First Amendment reflects this belief:

Congress shall make no law respecting an establishment of religion.

This is usually taken to mean not only that the government should not set up an established church; it should do nothing that even suggests support for a religion. In a letter to Madison, Thomas Jefferson once offered the hope that "the wall of separation" between church and state would always be kept high. So often have his words been quoted (sometimes in Supreme Court decisions) that many believe the phrase "wall of separation" is actually part of the Bill of Rights. It is not. However, the belief that church and state should be separate is at the heart of the First Amendment, and it is largely because of this amendment that the United States has developed into one of the world's most religiously diverse countries.

The establishment clause is not always easy to interpret, however. While required school prayer has been declared to be outside the Constitution, not all points of contact between government and religion have been. Congress itself, for example, begins its daily session with a prayer offered by a chaplain, and it pays the salaries of chaplains in the armed forces. Many people find this situation confusing.

The Supreme Court has usually taken the position that the key question where prayer is concerned is whether it is compulsory. In a public school situation, students have to be present, and even if individuals who object to prayer are allowed to leave the room, that very action sets them apart from other students in a way that may embarrass them. In Congress, on the other hand, members are present as a result of their own choice and are mature enough to make their own decisions.

Like many areas of the Constitution, the establishment clause is subject to different interpretations. While many hold that it requires a high "wall of separation" between church and state, others argue that it simply forbids a state church and requires that government treat all religions equally. According to this view, government aid to religion is all right as long as it is available to all religions on an equal basis.

Others, however, would disagree. A number of controversies have involved publicly financed Christmas decorations. The Supreme Court has said that a crèche (representing the manger and the Christ child) displayed in a public park with other decorations is permissible, since the overall effect is not primarily religious. In 1988, however, the Court ruled that a Nativity scene by itself on the steps of a county courthouse marked too close a relationship between church and state.

Controversies over the establishment clause are common when it comes to schools. One source of disagreement has been the fact that while all children are required to attend school, they are not all required to attend *public* schools. In many communities, church-related schools also exist. The question of whether such schools should be able to receive financial or other aid from state and local governments has been debated. Some believe that since church-related schools spare the taxpayers the cost of educating their pupils, church-related schools ought to be compensated. Others argue that any government assistance to church-related schools amounts to the state fostering religion.

The Supreme Court has usually sought a middle path through such arguments. It has generally found that government assistance that benefits students as individuals (such as the provision of bus transportation or school books) does not breach the "wall of separation," while aid that primarily benefits a church-related school, such as paying teachers' salaries, does breach that wall.

The Free Exercise Clause

The other part of the First Amendment's guarantee of freedom of religion is the free exercise clause:

Congress shall make no law respecting an establishment of religion, or the free exercise thereof.

These words were intended to protect the individual's freedom of conscience in religious matters and to safeguard a person's right to choose the form of religion (if any) that he or she would follow. In other words, the framers of the Bill of Rights wanted to guarantee toleration for a wide range of religious beliefs. The free exercise clause has therefore contributed to the diversity of religious beliefs and practice that typifies American society.

Like other parts of the Bill of Rights, the free exercise clause sounds clear and easy to understand. Yet it is not always so. Taken literally, the clause would protect any action that could in some way be related to religious belief. People could break laws or do whatever they wanted to do without fear of punishment, as long as they claimed that their actions were a way of practicing their religious beliefs. Such a situation, however, would clearly be unacceptable, either in James Madison's day or in modern society.

Therefore there must be limits to the exercise of religious freedom. The need to define these limits often occurs when a recognized religion approves of a practice that is contrary to the law or to widely held standards of public morality. In the nineteenth century, for example, the Church of Jesus Christ of

Church Membership Among Americans

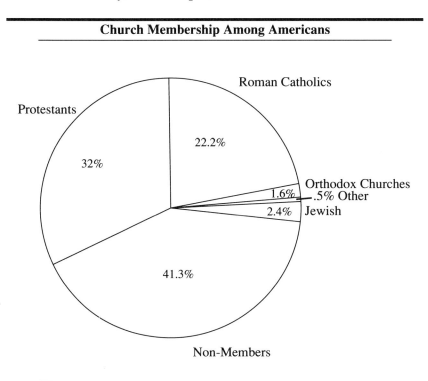

SOURCE: Data are from *The World Almanac and Book of Facts*, edited by Mark S. Hoffman (New York: Pharos Books, 1991), p. 610.

Latter-day Saints (the Mormons) condoned the practice of polygyny: Men could have more than one wife. The practice shocked and horrified other denominations and was illegal in all states and in federal territories. Claims that this religiously motivated polygyny was protected by the First Amendment were denied by the courts, and the issue created a long-drawn-out controversy between the Mormons and the federal government in the Utah Territory. Eventually the Mormons renounced the practice. Only then was Utah admitted to the Union.

More recently, the free exercise clause has been at the center of controversies involving the Native American Church and its use of peyote. The Native American Church combines Christian teaching and doctrine with many forms of religious expression that are traditional among native American Indian tribes. Visions have traditionally been important in Indian spiritual life, and various tribes have developed ways of inducing such visions. One way, practiced among some Indians since before Columbus, is to smoke peyote, which comes from some cactus plants. To members of the Native American Church, using peyote in this fashion is a sacrament. Peyote, however, is classified as a hallucinogen (a drug that causes hallucinations), and its use is against the law in many states, because under the influence of this drug a person could endanger his own life or the lives of others. Whose right should prevail: the right of a member of the Native American Church to exercise his religion or the state's right to protect its citizens from harmful substances?

Many states have dealt with the problem by exempting genuine members of the Native American Church from the laws against use of peyote. Not all have, however, nor do all permit the passage of peyote (which is primarily grown in Texas) across their state lines. There are other complications. In Oregon, two Native Americans lost their jobs when they

Some people argue that public display of a Christmas scene amounts to the State fostering religion. (Mark Reinstein/Uniphoto)

failed drug tests that showed they had used peyote, and they were denied unemployment benefits. (Generally speaking, people who lose their jobs for such reasons are not eligible for unemployment insurance.) They took their case to court. On appeal, the Supreme Court ruled against them.

Even though such questions remain controversial, the First Amendment continues to guarantee that Americans may worship wherever they wish — in a church, synagogue, mosque, temple, or other place — and prevents the government from preferring one over the others.

Chapter Four

Freedom
of
Expression

No symbol of the United States commands greater affection and respect than the American flag. American students begin their school day with the pledge of allegiance, and Americans are taught from childhood the proper ways to care for and display the flag. Mistreatment of the flag is likely to provoke emotional reaction. Until 1989, state and federal laws made it a crime to burn, tear, or otherwise show disrespect for the flag.

To people upset with the direction of government policy, however, the flag can seem a powerful symbol against which to protest. In 1984, Gregory Johnson protested against the policies of the Reagan Administration by burning a flag outside the Republican National Convention in Dallas. He was arrested under Texas' flag protection law. In 1989, the case made it to the Supreme Court. There, in a close 5-4 decision, the Court decided that burning the flag as an act of protest was a legitimate form of political expression and was entitled to the protection of the First Amendment's free speech clause.

There was much negative reaction to the Court's decision, and for a time it looked as if the Constitution might be amended to allow flag protection laws. (Such an action would have marked the first time in American history that the

Constitution had been amended to limit the scope of the First Amendment.) Efforts in Congress fell short, though the issue remains controversial.

What Is "Expression"?

The flag-burning cases raise important questions about the meaning of the First Amendment:

Congress shall make no law . . . abridging the freedom of speech

Why should people be able to express themselves in ways that a majority of Americans might find offensive? Why is "freedom of speech" interpreted to include nonverbal forms of expression?

James Madison and the other framers of the Constitution believed that freedom of speech was one of the most important characteristics of a free people. To Madison and his colleagues, free discussion was part of the pursuit of truth: It was absolutely necessary if citizens were to be able to make good choices among candidates or to develop informed opinions about public affairs. Some Supreme Court justices have thought freedom of expression so important that they have spoken of First Amendment rights as having a *preferred position* in the interpretation of the Constitution; that is, they have stated that when other rights come into conflict with First Amendment rights, the First Amendment will prevail, and that any law that seeks to limit First Amendment rights must have very powerful (or "compelling") reasons for doing so.

Though the free speech clause originally was applied primarily to spoken words, in the twentieth century it came to include other forms of expression as well. The words on a protester's sign, for example, are not spoken, but they are as much a form of political expression as a shouted slogan or a speech from a soapbox. Why should they be treated any differently?

The First Amendment's free speech clause guarantees the right to free political expression. (Sally Ann Rogers)

In the 1960's, the Court generally ruled that nonviolent demonstrations, such as sit-ins, could not be outlawed. Such actions are often classed as *symbolic speech*. On the other hand, the Court refused to extend the First Amendment's protection to cover the burning of draft cards as a form of protest. It is not always easy, even for judges, to tell where "freedom of speech" ends. Generally, the Court has taken the position that the form of expression used must emphasize expression over action. It also helps if the form of expression itself is legal (burning draft cards was not), though the flag-burning cases show that expression can sometimes lead to the overturning of laws.

The free speech clause was primarily intended to protect *political* expression, and the Court has extended its interpretation furthest in that direction. Free speech, however, has other meanings. One area of nonpolitical expression that is covered by the First Amendment is *commercial speech*. For many years, state laws allowed certain professional organizations, notably associations of doctors and lawyers, to prohibit advertising by their members. In the 1960's, some claimed that such restrictions amounted to a violation of their right to free speech. The Court agreed. Today, the advertising of medical and legal services seldom provokes comment.

Limitations on Free Speech

Just as the free speech clause has not been taken literally to mean only spoken words, the provision that Congress "make no law" has also been interpreted in a non-literal fashion. A person does not have a right to say absolutely anything and have his or her words protected by the First Amendment. Over the years, the Supreme Court has recognized certain circumstances in which Congress or state legislatures can restrict the meaning of the free speech clause. Since government can do little to prevent expression, limitations primarily take the form of penalties that may be applied after the fact.

One area that has provoked controversy is speech that is political in nature but also encourages people to break the law. During World War I, the Espionage and Sedition Acts were passed, making it a federal crime to encourage resistance to the draft or to express ideas that otherwise interfered with the war effort. Though some thought the acts went too far, the Supreme Court upheld them as constitutional. Justice Oliver Wendell Holmes pointed out that the right to free speech was not absolute. It did not extend, he said, to the right to shout "Fire!" in a crowded theater. Freedom of speech could be restricted if the expression of certain ideas posed a "clear and present danger" by advocating actions that Congress had a legitimate right to prohibit (in this case interference with the draft). Though the phrase "clear and present danger" has itself been given different interpretations, it has remained the basic test that must be met before political expression can be restricted.

Other categories of speech and expression also are not considered to be protected by the First Amendment. If one person makes a remark to another that he knows is likely to provoke a violent reaction, the provocation may fall under the heading of *fighting words*, a category of speech that is not covered by the free speech clause. Here again there are problems of definition. The Court defines the category of "fighting words" rather narrowly. Generally, such speech must be addressed to a specific individual and must be spoken with the purpose of provoking a strong reaction.

Two other types of non-protected expression are obscenity and defamation. (Here, as sometimes happens, definitions of freedom of speech and freedom of the press often overlap.) Obscenity has always been considered to be outside the scope of First Amendment protection. The real problem is to define what is, and is not, obscene. A dictionary might provide a definition of obscenity as expression that is dirty, lewd, or repulsive, but it is hard to apply such a definition in practice, because what is obscene to one person may seem to be artistic or political expression to another. One justice once expressed the problem by remarking that he knew obscenity when he saw it but that he could not define it.

During the 1960's and 1970's, the Court tended to adopt a broad definition that allowed a great range of expression. The debate continues today. In 1990, a record store owner in Florida was arrested for selling an album by the rap group 2 Live Crew, called *As Nasty as They Wanna Be*, on the grounds that its lyrics were obscene. He claimed that the album was a legitimate form of artistic expression and was entitled to the First Amendment's protection. Perhaps the best way to sum up the problem is simply to say that whatever the courts define as obscene is not protected by the Constitution.

Defamation is the use of words that are untrue and that tend to lower a person's reputation. If such words are spoken, they are called *slander*; if written, they are called *libel*. The law of defamation predates the Constitution and was developed to protect people from lies and malicious gossip. (Truth is a valid defense against a charge of slander or libel.) Defamation has never been considered as enjoying the First Amendment's protection. At times politicians have attempted to restrain the give-and-take of political debate by claiming that opponents or journalists are defaming them. To preserve free and public discussion of political issues, however, the courts have required public figures to prove not only that the statements about them were made without regard to truth, but also that they were made with malicious intent — that is, deliberately to harm the person's character and reputation. "Public figures" are further defined not just as politicians but as people in the public eye. Such people include celebrities. As "public figures," therefore, television and movie stars find it difficult to prosecute for libel when outlandish stories are printed about them.

Private citizens protest the policies of the president in Washington, D.C. (Susan Hormuth)

There are also certain types of institutions for which the courts recognize limits on freedom of expression: prisons, the military, and schools. For reasons that differ for each type of institution, the courts have tended to hold that these institutions have legitimate reasons for limiting freedom of expression. In the case of schools, some limitations are justified on the grounds that maintaining an environment suitable for learning is a basic necessity and that school officials are usually the best judges of how this can be achieved. Disruptive forms of expression that might be protected outside school will often not be protected on school grounds. The authority of school administrations to regulate expression is limited, however. In 1969, the Supreme Court ruled unconstitutional an attempt by the Des Moines school board to ban the wearing of black armbands as a protest against the Vietnam War.

Finally, the government may regulate the time, manner, and place of some forms of speech and expression. A group's right to demonstrate for a particular cause might be subject to restrictions limiting where and when the demonstration may take place. It might be banned from a hospital zone, for example. Such restrictions must not be based on the content of the demonstration, and government must treat all points of view the same way: If it keeps one group from demonstrating at a busy intersection during rush hour, it must apply the same rule to all groups.

Chapter Five

Freedom
of the
Press

In 1971, *The New York Times* obtained a copy of the "Pentagon Papers," a study done a few years earlier by the U.S. Department of Defense that detailed the steps leading to the United States' involvement in the Vietnam War. Although it contained no military secrets, the document was politically very sensitive. It showed that in many cases the government had not told the truth to the American people while the country's small advisory role in Vietnam had expanded to a massive military commitment. The government had classified the "Pentagon Papers" as secret.

After much discussion, the management of *The New York Times* decided to publish the "Pentagon Papers." After two installments, the federal government sued to prevent further publication on the grounds that to do so would endanger national security. In effect, the government was requesting that the courts allow it to censor *The New York Times*. The federal district court in New York agreed with the government. On appeal, however, the Supreme Court reversed the lower courts and allowed *The New York Times* to publish. The government, it ruled, had not proven a threat to national security that was strong enough to justify censorship.

A Free Press in a Free Society

The case of the "Pentagon Papers" is one of the most famous press freedom cases of the twentieth century and illustrates two central points in the American definition of a free press: The press has a special role to play in holding government accountable to the people, and in general there should be no prior censorship of the press. The press, however, may be held responsible for what it does publish.

Madison and the other framers of the Constitution were strong believers in a free press and staunch opponents of censorship. To them, a free society without a free press was a contradiction in terms. It was not just that printers and publishers had the same right as everyone else to speak their minds. Rather, they considered the press to be special: It played a crucial role as watchdog over the government. If those in office abused their power or acted dishonestly, the press was the institution most likely throw light on their misconduct. The press, in other words, was to function as an informal but important check on government. To perform this vital function, the press itself had to be largely free of government controls and restraints, especially with regard to censorship.

It was no accident that freedom of the press became part of the First Amendment. In the eighteenth century, a debate raged between those who shared the view that the press was a necessary watchdog and those who worried that the press would act irresponsibly and make it impossible for anyone to govern. At the time, the common law recognized the crime of *seditious libel*: Words that criticized government and encouraged disloyalty were considered to be illegal. In 1735, one of the most famous cases involving freedom of the press came to trial in New York, when John Peter Zenger, publisher of the *New York Weekly Journal*, was charged with seditious libel for criticizing the royal governor of the colony. In defiance of the judge's instructions, the jury acquitted Zenger. The case established two important precedents: Truth could be used as a defense against a charge of seditious libel, and the jury (rather than the judge) would determine whether the material was seditious.

Seditious libel did not go away, but it became increasingly difficult for the government to use it to silence criticism, especially after the unpopularity of the federal Sedition Act of 1798 backfired on those who had supported it. Though wars would often bring temporary restrictions on the press, American governments learned to live with press criticism.

Broadcast Media and the First Amendment

When the free press clause of the First Amendment was drafted, the press was largely limited to newspapers. The appearance of radio in the early twentieth century raised the question of whether the new medium should be included under the First Amendment's protection. The tendency of Congress and the courts was to answer that it should. Their actions set a precedent that was followed when television came along.

The broadcast media are covered by the constitutional guarantee of freedom of the press, but it is coverage with a difference. From the beginning, the broadcast media have been subjected to a greater degree of government regulation than have print media. The major reason for this lies in the physical nature of radio and television. Broadcast media use frequencies in the electromagnetic spectrum (the energy waves that make light, heat, and radio waves). The frequencies for sending radio and TV signals are limited in number. In the early days of radio, broadcasters would often shift from one frequency to another, jamming any station that might be operating on the same frequency. There were frequencies for only so many stations.

The government, which had licensed radio broadcasters from the beginning, stepped in. The Federal Radio Act of 1927

First Amendment Controversies

Issue	Reasons to Limit	Reasons Not to Limit
Does the First Amendment protect the right of members of the Native American Church to smoke peyote as part of their religious rituals?	Peyote is a controlled substance. To permit its use might endanger the lives of the user and others.	The free exercise of religion by the Native American Church requires the use of peyote. Freedom of religion should not be infringed.
Does the First Amendment protect the right of art galleries to display publicly artworks that may be considered obscene or offensive?	The First Amendment does not protect pornography or obscenity. If a work is considered offensive by people in the community, it should not be displayed.	Freedom of speech and freedom of the press imply free expression. Art is in the eye of the beholder.
Does the First Amendment protect those who burn the American flag in violation of state laws?	The flag is the country's most important symbol. State governments ought to be allowed to protect it.	Burning the flag is as legitimate an act of protest as speaking out against a government policy. Preventing flag-burning would be banning a form of political expression.
Should schools and public libraries ban books that contain racially offensive terms?	Use of some racial terms is offensive and may lower the self-esteem of minority students.	Censorship restricts the flow of ideas. Students would be prevented from reading literature that was written in a time when such terms were considered more acceptable.
Should the press be allowed to print any government documents?	The press's freedom should be restricted to ensure national security.	Government decisions should be exposed to the will of the people.
Should newspapers and the media be allowed access to participants in a trial before a verdict has been delivered?	Unlimited discussion of trial-related matters in a public forum may infringe upon Fifth Amendment rights to due process.	Matters of public concern should be open for discussion.

established a government agency, known since 1934 as the Federal Communications Commission (FCC), to assign frequencies and otherwise regulate the infant radio industry. When television made its appearance, it, too, fell within the FCC's jurisdiction. Since the number of applicants for licenses at times exceeds the number of available frequencies, the FCC has often been in the position of deciding who gets a license and who does not. Congress has further required that broadcast stations operate "in the public interest," and this is one of the standards the FCC uses in renewing station licenses.

Broadcast media thus are on different footing from newspapers. Government has never tried to limit the number of newspapers, and newspapers do not need licenses and are not required to operate in the public interest. Historically, government regulation has imposed two significant rules on the way broadcast media cover public affairs: the *equal-time requirement* and the *fairness doctrine*. The former requires that candidates for public office have equal access to the airways. If advertising time is given or sold to one candidate, it must be available to others on the same basis. The fairness doctrine required that stations make time available to individuals or groups that were criticized or attacked on the air and required that stations broadcasting editorials allow those with contrary views to air them. The result was that broadcast stations seldom took strong stands on controversial issues. The great expansion of FM radio and cable television, which offered many different outlets for expression, made the fairness doctrine seem less necessary to many, and the FCC officially set it aside in 1987. Many stations, however, continue to follow it.

Limitations on Press Freedom

While the press in general, and the print media in particular, enjoy the general freedom to publish or broadcast without censorship, freedom of the press, like other freedoms, has its limits. In the "Pentagon Papers" case, the Supreme Court was careful not to say that national security could never be valid grounds for prior censorship, and in 1984 a federal district court issued an order preventing publication of plans that showed how to construct a nuclear bomb.

Another area of controversy has been that of pretrial publicity. Here the press's First Amendment freedom sometimes comes into conflict with the Fifth Amendment's guarantee of due process. At times judges have sought to impose restrictions on what the press can publish before a case comes to trial. The Supreme Court has rarely let such actions stand if they take the form of outright censorship. Judges, however, have had more success with "gag orders" that instruct parties involved in a trial not to talk with the press, and they sometimes order that pretrial proceedings take place in private. Once something becomes a matter of legal record, however, there is little that can prevent publication.

While the press is generally free to publish without prior censorship, it may still be held legally responsible for what it does publish. Defamation and obscenity are not considered to be protected by the First Amendment. The distinction in libel cases between public figures and ordinary citizens is especially important in this regard. Here again *The New York Times* was involved in a precedent-setting case. In 1960, the paper ran an advertisement from a civil rights group criticizing the way state and local governments in Alabama had handled civil rights protests. L. B. Sullivan, one of the city commissioners in Montgomery, sued the paper for libel, charging that there were inaccuracies in the advertisement. The state courts found in his favor and ordered *The New York Times* to pay $500,000 in damages.

The case was appealed to the Supreme Court. In 1964, a unanimous Court overturned the decision of the Alabama courts. Though acknowledging inaccuracies in the ad, the

Court found no "reckless disregard for the truth" and no "presence of malice" toward Alabama officials. Public officials, it noted, must establish such conditions in order to prove defamation. *The New York Times v. Sullivan* became the landmark case that requires public figures to prove much more than ordinary citizens in order to use the law of libel as protection from untruths. To have ruled otherwise would have been to allow libel law to play much the same role as charges of seditious libel had in the eighteenth century. Requiring that public officials prove malicious intent provides much more freedom to the press and ensures that political debate remains free and wide open.

Not all publications are entitled to the First Amendment protections enjoyed by commercial newspapers and broadcast stations. Institutionally sponsored publications, such as school newspapers, are not considered to enjoy the full scope of the First Amendment. The key case here came in 1988, when the Court upheld the action of a St. Louis high school principal who had substituted two stories in the school paper for two he found objectionable. The Court ruled that educational concerns in such cases outweigh any student claim to "freedom of the press," and that school administrators were the people best situated to judge which educational concerns were essential.

Chapter Six

The Right
to
Due Process

Anyone who has seen a police show on television has witnessed this scene hundreds of times: A person suspected of committing a crime is arrested. The star of the show turns to his sidekick and remarks, "Read him his rights." The co-star produces his "Miranda card" and reads a warning that begins: "You have the right to remain silent. . . ." The suspect is then carted off to the police station.

Many television viewers are so used to this scene that they seldom notice it. It is a reminder, however, of the great importance that the framers of the Bill of Rights attached to the creation of safeguards against government abuse of the criminal law. Persons suspected of committing crimes definitely have rights, and a greater portion of the Bill of Rights — the Fourth through the Eighth Amendments — deals with the broad subject of individual rights as they relate to legal proceedings than to any other single subject. These five amendments contain a number of specific rights; their overall intention is to ensure that no person can be deprived of life, liberty, or property without due process of law.

What Is "Due Process"?

The guarantee of the right to due process appears in both the Fifth and the Fourteenth Amendments. Most interpretations of these provisions reflect the idea that before the government can bring its power to bear against an individual suspected or accused of a crime, it must act in ways that are fair, not arbitrary — that is, not unpredictable or inconsistent. Furthermore, a person cannot be presumed to be guilty before trial.

MIRANDA WARNING

1. You have the right to remain silent.
2. Anything you say can and will be used against you in a court of law.
3. You have the right to talk to a lawyer and have him present with you while you are being questioned.
4. If you cannot afford to hire a lawyer, one will be appointed to represent you before any questioning, if you wish one.

Police officers read these statements to any person they arrest, to make sure that person knows his rights.

SOURCE: Courtesy of the Clinton, Iowa, Police Department.

Those who insisted on the Bill of Rights feared arbitrary government power. They regarded abuse of the criminal law as the most likely form that government repression might take, and they were determined to prevent it. Their attitudes were shaped both by the long history of the English common law and by the events that preceded the American Revolution.

The origins of due process are often traced to Magna Carta, the great charter of concessions forced from England's King John by his barons in 1215. Magna Carta promised that no free man could be deprived of his life, freedom, or possessions except by the "law of the land" (that is, by established and recognized procedures, not merely by the king's will). Magna Carta was often cited by later generations of English subjects and colonial Americans as they sought to protect themselves from arbitrary actions. In fact, the Declaration of Independence justified the break with Britain partly on grounds that the Crown had departed from due process of law by employing dependent judges, removing cases from the localities in which they had originated, threatening the right to a trial by jury, and other unfair practices.

Due process, broadly defined, includes a whole cluster of rights. A number of these involve procedures that government must follow before it can bring a person to trial. These *pretrial rights*, in fact, affect more people than do those that involve trial and punishment. Most people questioned by the police are not arrested, and the majority of those arrested do not come to trial.

Certain pretrial rights were included in the main body of the Constitution itself: the right to *habeas corpus* (a legal procedure that requires the government to bring a suspect to court and either charge him with a crime or let him go, an important safeguard against imprisonment without trial), and the provisions that there will be no *ex post facto* laws (laws that make an act a crime after it has been committed) or *bills of attainder* (a process by which a person is declared guilty of a crime by legislative action).

Other important pretrial rights are found in the Bill of Rights. The Fourth Amendment provides that there shall be no unreasonable searches or seizures of property that could be used as evidence. Though the term "unreasonable" is open to interpretation, the courts have generally held it to mean that searches and seizures should be by means of a legally obtained search warrant. Searches without warrants are permitted only

"Due process" rights ensure that those arrested for a crime are innocent until tried and proven guilty in a court of law. (Grant/PhotoBank)

under certain conditions, such as with the owner's permission or if they immediately follow a lawful arrest.

The Fifth Amendment's protection against self-incrimination and the Sixth Amendment's right to counsel (legal representation) also shape pretrial proceedings. Their importance was established by the case that produced the famous Miranda warning. Ernesto Miranda was arrested by police in Phoenix, Arizona, for kidnapping and rape. He confessed to the crime before consulting a lawyer. He later appealed his conviction on the grounds that he was unaware that he did not have to talk to police or that he could have a lawyer provided for him by the state. In 1966, the Supreme Court reversed Miranda's conviction, holding that the circumstances of his confession amounted to self-incrimination and denial of the right to counsel. The Miranda warning became a permanent part of police procedure.

Protection against self-incrimination and the right to counsel are also among the many rights that protect the accused once a case actually goes to trial. Defendants, for example, cannot be forced to testify against themselves. Trial by jury itself is one of the oldest and most highly prized rights a defendant in a criminal trial can claim and one that is safeguarded by the Sixth Amendment. The amendment also provides that the trial must be speedy, public, and local — it should take place within the district where the crime was committed. (The location, or *venue*, of the trial may be changed, however, if the judge thinks that the defendant will not receive a fair trial in a particular community.) These provisions were included in the Bill of Rights to prevent government from secretly operating against individuals. Community vigilance was seen as a check on the government.

Defendants in criminal cases are also protected against *double jeopardy* (being tried twice for the same offense), and they have the right to confront witnesses against them, as well as the right to *subpoena* witnesses for their defense. (A subpoena is a legal order requiring that a person or piece of evidence be present at a trial.) If convicted, defendants are protected from "cruel and unusual punishments." The meaning of this last phrase has been debated.

Due Process Controversies

Few areas of constitutional rights have been as marked by controversy in the second half of the twentieth century as the area of due process. In the 1950's, the Supreme Court began to examine criminal justice procedures more closely and paid greater attention to the rights of those accused of crimes. Judicial interpretations, as in the Miranda case, often overturned convictions. Since the country was at the same time experiencing a marked increase in crime, some believed that the Court was interpreting the Constitution so as to "coddle criminals." Two areas proved especially controversial: the introduction of the exclusionary rule and the question of whether capital punishment was cruel and unusual punishment.

Probably no court-related requirement seemed to complicate the lives of law enforcement officers more than the *exclusionary rule*. The rule, which the Court began to apply in 1961 with a decision in *Mapp v. Ohio*, holds that evidence obtained unconstitutionally may not be used in court, and convictions based on such evidence may be overturned, as in the Miranda case. The rule is most applicable to searches and confessions. Searches must adhere strictly to the ever-evolving interpretation of the Fourth Amendment. The area of unwarranted searches has proven to be particularly complicated. In the case of automobiles, for example, the Court has ruled that a stopped car can be searched if there is something illegal in "plain view" or if a police officer has probable cause to believe that one or more of the occupants

Those accused of a crime have the right to a trial by a jury of their peers. (Billy E. Barnes/ Uniphoto)

committed a crime. On the other hand, "fishing expeditions" (when police stop cars simply because they might find something incriminating) are unconstitutional. "Probable cause" also means different things to different people. Generally the Court has taken the view that "looking suspicious" is not enough. The Court has also ruled that school administrators may search student lockers without probable cause.

In some cases, the exclusionary rule appeared to let vicious criminals go free because of technical irregularities in search warrants, unwarranted searches the courts would not accept, or confessions that did not follow the Miranda guidelines. Such examples prompted loud public outcries and helped to elect politicians who promised to "crack down on crime." Probably no topic illustrates so vividly the potential conflict between individual rights and public opinion. Supporters of the exclusionary rule point out that the Anglo-American legal tradition holds that it is better that the guilty go free than an innocent person be punished and that the rule is an effective check on police procedure. In addition, research supports the view that few criminals escape the law through technicalities.

Capital punishment has been another area of controversy. In 1972, the Supreme Court temporarily halted executions in the United States. In *Furman v. Georgia* it ruled that the death penalty had been applied in the past in such an inconsistent and arbitrary fashion that it amounted to cruel and unusual punishment. It did not, however, say that capital punishment itself was contrary to the Eighth Amendment. States wishing to retain the death penalty revised their laws to provide clear descriptions of the situations in which capital punishment would apply, usually also requiring that juries deliberate separately on the verdict (guilty or not guilty) and the penalty (punishment) in capital cases. In 1976, the Court upheld Georgia's new capital punishment law.

Though executions began again, the controversy continued. To some, the death penalty seemed a barbaric relic of the past, a penalty that had been abandoned by most other democracies. Others felt that those on death row still had too many opportunities to appeal their sentences and clogged the courts. The Court continued to hold that capital punishment was constitutional if fairly administered and deferred to the states on the question of whether it should exist.

Chapter Seven

Voting Rights

During the American Revolution, eleven states adopted new constitutions, often broadening voting rights in the process. New Jersey's new constitution was unique, however: All inhabitants worth fifty pounds (in British money) could claim the right to vote. This opened the vote to groups barred from voting in most other states, particularly women and blacks. Members of these groups voted in small numbers in New Jersey — until 1807. Responding to fears that women might decide close elections, particularly after some voted in a close contest in Hunterdon County, the state legislature passed an act that limited voting to white men. It would be more than sixty years before blacks voted again in New Jersey, and more than a century before women did.

New Jersey's early experiment with a relatively open suffrage illustrates a number of points about voting rights. First, it is a reminder that for many years, the states determined who could — and who could not — vote. Second, it shows that the right to vote was more likely to be limited than other rights, such as freedom of religion or freedom of speech: It was not necessarily believed that a person needed the right to vote in order to be considered free. Only gradually did a connection between voting rights and citizenship develop.

The States and Voting Rights

The Constitution adopted in 1789 said little about the right to vote and addressed the subject only as far as elections to the

House of Representatives were concerned. (The Senate was elected by state legislatures until 1913, and the method of choosing presidential electors was left to the states.) Members of Congress were to be chosen by the people of the several states, and the right to vote in congressional elections in each state was to be the same as in elections for the largest house of the state legislature. The Bill of Rights said nothing at all about voting rights.

From the late eighteenth century through the Civil War, state legislatures had complete control over the definition of voting rights, with results that differed in detail from state to state. None of them saw the right to vote as essential to citizenship. Property qualifications had been universal in colonial times, and many states kept these eligibility requirements after independence. Some states adopted a taxpayer qualification, but since taxes were largely based on ownership of property, such laws amounted to indirect property qualifications. Most states limited the vote entirely to whites, and (with the exception of New Jersey until 1807) all states restricted voting to adult males. Voting rights were thus limited to a definite minority of the adult population.

During the first two-thirds of the nineteenth century, the right to vote was broadened, at least for white males. Many of the newer states adopted laws calling for *manhood suffrage*, giving adult white males the right to vote as one of the rights of citizenship, and many of the original states followed suit. In most cases, though, voting rights continued to be restricted to white males: Only in some of the New England states were blacks allowed to vote on the same basis as whites, and New Jersey ended its brief experiment with woman suffrage in 1807. Still the growth of white male suffrage increased the electorate significantly. At the same time, it strengthened the association of voting rights with the rights of citizenship.

Constitutional Amendments and Voting Rights

During the Civil War era, Congress and the Constitution began to play an important role in defining voting rights. In the period of Reconstruction that followed the war, Congress required the former Confederate states to allow former slaves to vote on the same basis as whites. The Fourteenth

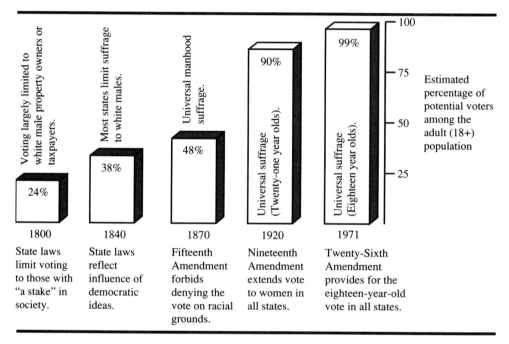

1800	1840	1870	1920	1971
State laws limit voting to those with "a stake" in society.	State laws reflect influence of democratic ideas.	Fifteenth Amendment forbids denying the vote on racial grounds.	Nineteenth Amendment extends vote to women in all states.	Twenty-Sixth Amendment provides for the eighteen-year-old vote in all states.

Amendment, ratified in 1868, called for reducing the representation in Congress of any state that denied the vote to any group of adult male citizens. Though this provision has never been used, it marked the first time that any constitutional amendment had attempted to define voting rights.

The Fifteenth Amendment, ratified in 1870, was more direct. It provided that no state could deny the right to vote on the basis of race, color, or previous status as a slave. One of its aims was to safeguard the voting rights of former slaves.

However, it was also intended to *enfranchise* (give the vote to) African Americans in the North, where the majority of states still restricted the vote to whites.

The Fifteenth Amendment set an important precedent for constitutional recognition of voting rights. It was not very successful, however, in safeguarding the voting rights of former slaves. Its language said that states could not deny the right to vote *on the basis of race*. This wording implied that voting rights could be denied on other bases, however. By 1900, most southern and border states had devised a variety of techniques for getting around the Fifteenth Amendment and preventing large numbers of blacks from voting: poll taxes, literacy tests (which were often administered unfairly), and all-white party primaries. Not until the second half of the twentieth century would Congress move to enforce the intent of the Fifteenth Amendment.

The Fifteenth Amendment did provide an important precedent for enfranchising a large group of citizens by constitutional amendment. This eventually became the goal of the women's suffrage movement. Originally it had followed a state-by-state approach, but this proved disappointing. In the early twentieth century, the movement began to work for securing a women's suffrage amendment. After much effort, it succeeded. In 1920, the states ratified the Nineteenth Amendment, which provided that the right to vote could not be denied on the basis of sex.

During and after World War II, African Americans began to organize and work against the various forms of racial discrimination that they faced. The vote became an important weapon in this struggle. In order for blacks in the southern and border states to vote, however, the various techniques that had blocked implementation of the Fifteenth Amendment would have to be eliminated. Since the Democratic Party was politically dominant in much of the South, the Democratic primary that selected the party's candidates was the only election that mattered. Excluding blacks from the primary was an effective way of depriving them of the vote. In 1944, the Supreme Court declared such all-white primaries illegal.

Another popular technique for keeping African Americans (as well as many poor whites) from voting was the poll tax. In order to vote, a person had to pay a poll tax, keep the payments up to date, and produce written records proving that all this had been done. Under the influence of the Civil Rights movement, the Twenty-Fourth Amendment was ratified in 1964, banning the poll tax in federal elections.

The Voting Rights Act of 1965 was as effective as any court decision or amendment in protecting minority voting rights. This measure passed after the famous march from Selma to Montgomery, Alabama, led by Dr. Martin Luther King, Jr. The Voting Rights Act suspended literacy tests and allowed the appointment of federal registrars in counties where African Americans were not registered in numbers proportional to their presence in the local population. In addition, interference with a person's right to vote became a federal crime. Millions of southern blacks registered to vote in the wake of the act, and hundreds were elected to public office. The act was subsequently amended to provide protection for other minorities, especially Native Americans and Hispanic Americans. The Voting Rights Act remains the major federal law in this area, though it is subject to renewal every ten years.

At the same time that the Civil Rights movement was hitting its peak, the oldest members of the "Baby Boom" generation (those born between 1946 and 1963) were beginning to come of age. The era was marked by a greater consciousness of the importance of youth. Partly because of this, the Twenty-Sixth Amendment was proposed and ratified in 1971. This amendment established a national voting age of eighteen.

The right to vote by secret ballot is aided by new technology. (Billy E. Barnes/Uniphoto)

Voting Rights Today

Voting rights are much more widely held among the American people of today than they were when New Jersey took the vote away from women and blacks in 1807. Today the Fifteenth, Nineteenth, Twenty-Fourth, and Twenty-Sixth Amendments, together with the Voting Rights Act, have made the definition of voting rights more a federal than a state responsibility.

This development has been supported by the federal courts, which have increasingly taken the viewpoint that voting rights are closely associated with other basic civil rights. Even in the matter of residency qualifications (requiring that a person live in a particular state or locality for a set period of time), the courts have left the states with little leeway in setting requirements for the vote. In a country where people move as often as Americans tend to move, residency requirements can pose a problem for many would-be voters. Once requirements that a person live in a state for two years were common. Today, the courts are likely to judge any period of more than thirty days as unconstitutional. The largest groups of adults that states may still keep from voting are those convicted of serious crimes, the mentally incompetent, and the homeless.

Court decisions have not only helped to extend voting rights; They have also made many people's votes more important. In a series of cases in the 1960's, the Supreme Court ruled that state legislatures and congressional districts must be of approximately the same size (the "one-person, one-vote" standard). Prior to this, voters in urban areas often found themselves in much larger districts and, thus, underrepresented in legislative bodies at both the state and national levels.

The Constitution, Congress, and the courts have done much to expand and enlarge the American electorate. The one thing they have not been able to do is inspire Americans to vote. As the number of those eligible to vote has increased, the proportion of those who do vote has been declining. Today the United States has one of the lowest rates of voter participation among democratic countries.

Chapter Eight

Equality
Under the Law

Before World War II, Gunnar Myrdal, a Swedish sociologist, began an investigation of the state of race relations in the United States. The result of his research was published in 1944 as *An American Dilemma*. In the book, Myrdal identified a contradiction that he saw at the heart of American life: Americans professed a strong commitment to the ideal of equality set forth in the Declaration of Independence, but at the same time Americans of African descent were forced into a subordinate position.

The war then raging underlined Myrdal's point. The United States and its allies were fighting for freedom and democracy against an openly racist enemy, Adolf Hitler's Germany, but the army was segregated along racial lines and 120,000 Americans of Japanese ancestry (two-thirds of them native-born citizens) were interned in camps.

These characteristics of World War II highlight the gap between American ideals and American practice in matters of race. For more than two centuries, the multiracial composition of American society has posed a major challenge to American values of freedom, equality, and democracy. Few areas of American life have given more meaning to the concept of equal rights. This has been especially true of the experience of African Americans. In fact, to many Americans the term

Racism threatens to destroy the equality guaranteed by law. (Mark Reinstein/Uniphoto)

"civil rights" brings to mind images of the black struggle for equality.

Race and the Constitution

In the eighteenth century, the framers of the Constitution did not concern themselves specifically with the question of race, though they paid much attention to the question of slavery. In various ways, the Constitution protected slavery: The international slave trade could not be ended until 1808, owners were to be able to recapture runaway slaves, and slaves were included in the determination of congressional apportionment (though not at the same rate as the free population). Had such provisions not been included, there would probably have never been a Constitution. The great majority of African Americans then lived in the South, and most of them were slaves. The details of race relations were left to the states. While slaves were given few rights at all, free blacks also suffered lack of equality — even in the northern states that had abolished slavery or had never had it. In fact, it was in the North where states first required racial segregation in many areas of life, such as public transportation and education. Such segregation would later be called a "Jim Crow" system. Only in northern New England did free blacks approach equality with whites.

In 1857, the situation became worse when the Supreme Court put its stamp of approval on this widespread racial inequality. In the *Dred Scott* decision, Chief Justice Roger Taney said that, under the Constitution, blacks "had no rights which the white man was bound to respect" and that persons of African descent — even if free — were not citizens of the United States.

From this low point, the constitutional position of African Americans changed rapidly. The Civil War and the Thirteenth Amendment (ratified in late 1865) ended slavery. Congress sought to protect the basic civil rights of the former slaves by passing the nation's first Civil Rights Act in 1866. This act recognized that former slaves had such basic rights as the rights to move, to make contracts, and to a bring suit in a court of law. Unsure about the Supreme Court's support for such measures and angry at attempts in some southern states to restrict black rights, Congress then moved to amend the Constitution to place protection of civil rights on a higher level. The result was the Fourteenth Amendment, ratified in 1868.

Never before had a part of the Constitution used the word "equal" in the context of defining rights. No part of the Constitution would be more important than the Fourteenth Amendment in shaping modern concepts of equal rights. The amendment did a number of other things. One was to provide a constitutional definition of citizenship for the first time. It declared that all persons (except Indians) born or naturalized in the United States were citizens of the United States and of the state in which they lived. This effectively overturned the *Dred Scott* decision. Furthermore, the amendment provided that *states* could not limit the "privileges and immunities" of American citizens, deprive them of due process, or deny to anyone within their jurisdiction the "equal protection" of the laws. The Fourteenth Amendment also contained a section authorizing Congress to enforce it through appropriate legislation.

Supporters of the Fourteenth Amendment believed not only that it would provide constitutional support for the Civil Rights Act, but also that it would allow the various protections in the Bill of Rights to be used to prevent the states from abusing the rights of former slaves and other citizens. In some respects, the framers of the Fourteenth Amendment were thinking of civil rights in a new way. Traditionally, rights had been thought of as principles that limited the power of government — that told the government what it could *not* do. While the Fourteenth Amendment did not abandon this approach, it went beyond it and allowed citizens to call on the power of the federal government to protect their rights from being threatened by other citizens or by state government.

Though the Fourteenth Amendment would have enormous

U.S. Population by Ethnic Background

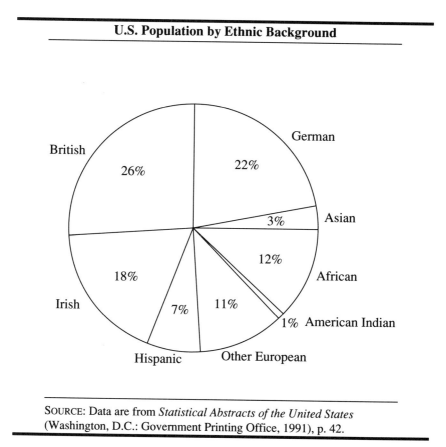

SOURCE: Data are from *Statistical Abstracts of the United States* (Washington, D.C.: Government Printing Office, 1991), p. 42.

influence on the future, its short-term impact was weaker than its supporters had hoped. A series of Supreme Court decisions narrowed its scope and refused to accept the view that the Fourteenth Amendment "incorporated" the Bill of Rights as a protection against the states. The climax of this line of reasoning came in 1896, when the Court handed down its decision in the case of *Plessy v. Ferguson*. This case centered on a Louisiana law that required separate railroad coaches for white and black passengers. Despite evidence that separate facilities left African Americans with inferior facilities, the Court upheld the Louisiana railroad law, establishing the principle of "separate but equal": States might require racial segregation as long as some effort at equal facilities were made. In practice, there was much more emphasis on "separate" than on "equal."

By the time of World War I, the United States was more racially segregated than it had ever been. In some thirty states, public schools were segregated along racial lines, and in the southern and border states full-blown systems of Jim Crow segregation kept blacks and whites apart in almost every area of life. The situation was much the same a few years later, when Gunnar Myrdal did the research for his 1944 book.

During World War II, the modern Civil Rights movement began to take shape: African Americans and sympathetic whites began to oppose racial discrimination more actively. One effective tactic, employed by the National Association for the Advancement of Colored People (NAACP), was to use the federal courts as a way of reviving the Fourteenth Amendment. The tactic was more successful in the post-World War II period than it would have been a generation earlier. Public opinion polls revealed that more and more white Americans were expressing a belief in racial equality. The 1920's and 1930's had seen the Supreme Court begin the "incorporation" of the Bill of Rights into the Fourteenth Amendment.

For a while, the Court appeared to be trying to improve life for African Americans by emphasizing that if facilities were separate, they must actually be of equal quality. Then, in 1954, the Court handed down one of its most important decisions in the case of *Brown v. Board of Education of Topeka, Kansas*, in which the NAACP had challenged the constitutionality of segregated schools. A unanimous Court ruled that separate schools would always be unequal and that such arrangements violated the Fourteenth Amendment. After fifty-eight years, the principle of "separate but equal" was dead. A series of Court decisions affecting wide areas of American life would follow.

Parallel to the NAACP's legal strategy, a number of important developments took place. Executive actions by Presidents Franklin D. Roosevelt and Harry S. Truman began to chip away at segregation and discrimination in defense hiring, the armed forces, and the federal government itself. Most important of all, the Civil Rights movement developed as a grass-roots movement, mobilizing millions of African Americans and their allies to work for change and equality. Led by Dr. Martin Luther King, Jr., and others, the Civil Rights movement proved impossible for political leaders to ignore.

After some limited measures were passed in 1957 and 1960, Congress in 1964 moved to fulfill the promise of the Fourteenth Amendment's enforcement section by passing a comprehensive Civil Rights Act. The Civil Rights Act of 1964 banned discrimination in public accommodations (businesses that serve the general public, such as restaurants and hotels), allowed the federal government to sue in order to hasten the desegregation of schools, made discrimination in employment on the basis of race or sex illegal, and allowed for the cut-off of federal funds to any program that operated in a discriminatory manner. The act immediately became, and has remained, the nation's primary civil rights law. In 1968, it was strengthened by an act that forbids discrimination in the sale or rental of housing.

Our society is racially and culturally diverse; recognition of our common bond as human beings will strengthen the social contract that guarantees equality under the law. (Joe Sohm/Chromosohm/Uniphoto)

Unfinished Business

By the mid-1960's, acts of Congress and Supreme Court decisions had made illegal virtually all forms of racial segregation and discrimination that had once been required by state law (also called *de jure segregation*). These measures had not solved the nation's racial problems, however. Much racial inequality remained (and remains) in American life, especially in terms of wealth, living conditions, and educational opportunities. There was (and is) much racial separation in the form of *de facto segregation* (segregation that exists in fact though not required by law). De facto segregation has proven a much tougher nut to crack, and the courts have ruled that such segregation is not unconstitutional if it is not the result of actions that were intended to promote segregation.

Attempts to promote greater equality have often proved to be very controversial. Busing students to promote racial balance in schools (often on the orders of federal courts) has often had the effect of causing white families to move to the suburbs, with the result that inner-city schools have "resegregated." In many of the nation's largest cities, schools today are as segregated as they were before the *Brown* decision.

Attempts to compensate for past discrimination and provide wider educational and employment opportunities to blacks and other minorities have led to *affirmative action* programs, in which minority members are recruited or are given some form of preference. Such programs have proven very controversial, especially where they are characterized by *racial quotas*: the setting aside of a specified number of places for minority candidates, regardless of whether they are the most qualified applicants. Some have charged that this practice amounts to *reverse discrimination*. In a landmark 1978 case, *Regents of the University of California v. Bakke*, which involved admission of a student to a medical school, the Supreme Court ruled that while race might be used as a factor in deciding whom to admit, outright quotas are unconstitutional. The whole question of affirmative action continues to be debated.

Defining the meaning of equal rights has also proved difficult and has often provoked conflict. While the African-American experience has been central to this struggle, other groups — such as women, Native Americans, Hispanics, and Asian Americans — have borne the burden of unequal treatment and have lent their support to broadening the meaning of "equality."

Chapter Nine

People
Who Made a
Difference

Civil rights, like other rights, have little meaning as theories or abstract ideas. For a right to exist, real people must be able to use it. Lawyers and judges have been important in defining civil rights, but legal professionals do not live and work in a vacuum. Ordinary people have also been crucial to the process. By claiming rights that others would deny them, people from many different backgrounds have expanded the meaning of civil rights for all Americans.

Fred Korematsu

Fred Korematsu was born in 1919 in California to parents who had come to the United States from Japan. Korematsu became a welder in a shipyard. His life seemed normal enough until the Japanese attacked Pearl Harbor on December 7, 1941.

In the aftermath of the bombing of Pearl Harbor, the Pacific coast states were panicked at the prospect of a Japanese attack. Many became convinced that the Japanese Americans who lived largely in the coastal states might gather intelligence for the enemy or commit acts of sabotage. (The government was never able to prove a single instance of sabotage or aid to the enemy.) Responding to political pressure and the argument that

As a Japanese American, Fred Korematsu was interned during World War II. (Rick Rocamora)

such an action was a "military necessity," on February 19, 1942, President Franklin D. Roosevelt signed Executive Order 9066, which authorized the army to intern Japanese Americans in camps. These American citizens were considered "security risks."

Japanese-American families had little time to dispose of their property before reporting for assignment to internment camps, which were generally located in isolated inland regions. Some 120,000 Japanese Americans (approximately two-thirds of them American citizens) were placed in camps.

A few Japanese Americans sought to avoid internment. Fred Korematsu was one. He tried to join the Navy but was turned down for medical reasons. He then underwent plastic surgery to look less Asian, hoping to stay and marry his white fiancée. He was arrested instead. Korematsu decided to go to court to fight internment. The American Civil Liberties Union (ACLU) offered him assistance. Korematsu argued that he was a loyal American and that internment would amount to a violation of due process, imprisoning him without trial. The case went all the way to the Supreme Court. There, in 1944, the Court in a 6-3 vote upheld his conviction.

As a result, Fred Korematsu came out of World War II with a criminal record that he felt was undeserved. Eventually he took the lead in winning vindication for Japanese Americans. Normally, once a case is decided by the Supreme Court, it is over for good. However, federal law allows those who have been convicted of crimes and who have served their sentences to clear their records if they can prove misconduct by the prosecution in their original trials. In 1981, Fred Korematsu obtained the government files from his case and brought suit, claiming that the government had suppressed evidence that would have brought the whole "military necessity" argument into question. In 1983, the federal district court in San Francisco vacated (annulled) his conviction. In a broader acknowledgment of error, Congress voted in 1988 to pay damages to Japanese Americans who had suffered internment.

Thurgood Marshall

Thurgood Marshall, a descendant of African slaves, was born in Baltimore in 1908. He was graduated first in his class from Howard University Law School in 1933. He became active in the NAACP and came to the attention of Charles H. Houston. Houston, a leading African-American lawyer, pioneered the NAACP's strategy of challenging racial discrimination on legal grounds, hoping to restore the Fourteenth Amendment's intended power. Eventually Marshall succeeded Houston as the NAACP's chief lawyer.

Of all the cases in which Thurgood Marshall was involved, the most important was *Brown v. Board of Education of Topeka, Kansas*, the case that overturned the old "separate but equal" standard that legalized segregation. Marshall coordinated the strategy that brought the case before the Supreme Court, directed the research that supported the NAACP's position, and then argued the case before the Court. Once the decision was handed down — "the doctrine of 'separate but equal' has no place" — Marshall worked to ensure its implementation.

Marshall's success at the NAACP won him much respect and attention. In 1961, President John F. Kennedy named him to the federal appeals court, and in 1965 President Lyndon B. Johnson appointed him Solicitor General. (The Solicitor General represents the United States government in cases before the Supreme Court.) Then, in 1967, Johnson appointed Thurgood Marshall to the Supreme Court. He was the first African American ever to sit on the nation's highest court.

As a Supreme Court justice, Marshall was a champion not only of minority rights but also of free speech and civil rights in general. He constantly reminded the Court of the need to

Thurgood Marshall, Supreme Court justice. (Library of Congress)

take into account the human consequences of its decisions, especially as they affected the poor, and he was an outspoken opponent of the death penalty. As the Court took a more conservative turn, Marshall found himself in the minority, yet even when the Court did not go along with his views, he remained a forceful presence. His dissents, especially on cases that sought to define the meaning of the equal protection clause, often influenced subsequent decisions.

Justice Marshall retired in 1991. He left behind a large legacy. Few justices have come to the Court with a legal career that can match Marshall's in terms of its constitutional importance. On the Court he continued to battle for equal rights. His is one of the great legal careers of the twentieth century.

Rosa Parks

Rosa Parks was born in 1904 in Alabama. Unlike many of her contemporaries in the black community, she was able to stay in school and graduate from high school. She found few challenging job opportunities, however, and eventually she went to work as a seamstress in a Montgomery department store. Feeling the pain of racial discrimination, she joined the local chapter of the NAACP and became its secretary, winning a reputation for efficient and high-quality work.

In the summer of 1955, she won a scholarship to the Highlander Folk School in Monteagle, Tennessee. Highlander was a unique institution. Its founder, Myles Horton, had established it to offer opportunities for interracial contact at a time when the Jim Crow system still dominated life in the South. Its workshops trained men and women to work against segregation and discrimination upon their return to their home communities. At Highlander, Rosa Parks learned that blacks and whites could live together on a basis of equality.

In 1955, Montgomery was one of the most segregated cities in the South, and its African-American community was denied access to equality in almost every phase of life. The public transit system typified the situation. The city required the separation of bus passengers on the basis of race, using a system that required blacks to fill in from the back of the bus and whites to fill in from the front. When the bus was filled, passengers in the front row of black seats were expected to give up their seats to new white passengers and stand in the rear.

On December 1, 1955, Rosa Parks had a tiring day at her job and took her seat for the bus ride home. As the bus filled, the driver asked her to move to the rear. She refused and was arrested. The black community rallied to her support. A boycott of the bus company was organized, led by a young Baptist minister who had only recently arrived in Montgomery: Martin Luther King, Jr. African Americans walked or traveled in car pools, and the boycott deprived the bus company of many of its most regular customers. A suit followed, challenging the city's bus segregation law. In 1956, the Supreme Court vindicated Rosa Parks by ruling the city law unconstitutional. After 382 days, the boycott came to an end. By keeping her seat, Rosa Parks had stood up for equal rights. She had also helped to launch a new phase of the Civil Rights movement, one that challenged inequality through nonviolent confrontation.

Clarence Earl Gideon

Clarence Gideon was born in Hannibal, Missouri, in 1910. After an unhappy childhood, he dropped out of school and left home. Gideon drifted around the country, working at odd jobs and engaging in small-time crime. He was arrested and jailed on a number of occasions.

In 1961, he was arrested again in Panama City, Florida, and charged with breaking into a pool hall. Gideon could not afford to hire a lawyer. When his case came to trial, the judge denied Gideon's request for a lawyer, pointing out that the state was required to furnish a lawyer only in capital cases (cases that might result in the death penalty). Gideon had to conduct his own defense. He was convicted and received the maximum sentence of five years in prison.

Clarence Gideon maintained his innocence and felt that he had been wronged when the court denied his request for legal counsel. In the library of the state prison, Gideon studied the law and decided to make an appeal to the Supreme Court. He drew up the brief himself, writing it in pencil on lined paper. His spelling was not always perfect, but Gideon put together a good argument. He said that the Sixth Amendment guaranteed the right to counsel, and defendants were unlikely to receive a fair trial unless assisted by a lawyer. To the surprise of many, in 1963 the Court agreed to hear Gideon's case.

The case, *Gideon v. Wainwright*, came at a time when the right-to-counsel clause was at a crucial stage of interpretation. Originally the "right to counsel" had meant the right to *hire* a lawyer, and the Sixth Amendment had applied only to federal cases. During the 1930's, the Court had begun to apply the Sixth Amendment to the states, requiring that counsel be provided for poor defendants in capital cases. In 1942, the right to have counsel supplied had been extended to a narrow range of other defendants, mostly those who were illiterate or mentally incompetent. Much controversy had developed around cases like Gideon's, in which the defendant was too poor to hire a lawyer but was also literate and aware of what was happening.

When the case was argued before the Supreme Court, Gideon did have a lawyer. The Supreme Court had a tradition of appointing skilled lawyers to assist poor defendants who appeared before it, and the Court had named Abe Fortas, a future Supreme Court justice, to represent Gideon. Fortas argued the case forcefully. In a unanimous decision, the Court

ruled that Gideon had a constitutional right to counsel that had been denied. A new trial, which acquitted him, was ordered. More important, a precedent was set that required that counsel be provided for all defendants accused of a felony.
Subsequently, the Court extended this right to anyone accused of a crime carrying a prison sentence. One man, armed with a pencil in a prison library, had shown that individual actions do define civil rights.

Mary Beth Tinker

Mary Beth Tinker was born in Burlington, Iowa, in 1952, the daughter of a Methodist minister. Both of her parents were active in the Civil Rights movement in the 1950's and 1960's, and both lost jobs as a result. They held fast to their beliefs, however, and they supported their children whenever they took a stand.

In 1965, the Tinkers were living in Des Moines, and Mary Beth had become involved in a group of students from different schools who were beginning to oppose the Vietnam War. On December 16, 1965, she wore a black armband to her eighth-grade classes at Harding Junior High. A few days before, the Des Moines school board had responded to rumors of the planned protest by enacting a rule that no armbands could be worn in the city's schools. Mary Tinker was taken out of her algebra class and was suspended from school; so were students at other schools who wore armbands that day.

At a school board meeting before a large crowd a few days later, a lawyer from the Iowa branch of the American Civil Liberties Union asked the board to repeal its ban on armbands, arguing that the rule amounted to an unconstitutional restriction on students' right of free expression. The board refused, and the ACLU took the case to court. (Mary Beth Tinker took off her armband and returned to school after the Christmas holidays.) By 1969 the case had worked its way to the Supreme Court.

Tinker v. Des Moines raised important questions about civil rights. Was wearing an armband "symbolic speech" protected by the First Amendment? Even if it was, could such expression be restricted in a school situation? Tinker's lawyers argued that wearing an armband was a protected form of political expression and that students did not leave their civil rights at the school door. The school board admitted that the armbands had not been disruptive and that it had permitted other forms of political expression in the past.

The Supreme Court decided the case in Tinker's favor by a 7-2 majority. It reaffirmed the view that the First Amendment protects expression beyond pure speech. It also found that, while the right of students to free expression was not unlimited during their time at school, such symbolic forms of protest were neither disruptive nor out of place. The action of a junior high school student had helped to extend the meaning of the First Amendment.

Chapter Ten

Outlook for the Future

December 15, 1991, marked the two hundredth anniversary of the ratification of the Bill of Rights. As the United States entered its third century of constitutionally protected freedom, American civil rights seemed likely to provide a model for other countries. At the same time, the process of defining civil rights seemed likely to remain controversial.

Influence Abroad

Outside the United States, the American Bill of Rights has seldom been as influential and inspirational as it was in the late 1980's and early 1990's. The destruction of the Berlin Wall on November 9, 1989, symbolized a widespread desire to share the rights that Americans often take for granted, and new governments across Eastern Europe and the nations that once formed the Soviet Union promised recognition of the rights necessary to democracy: freedom of religion, freedom of expression, freedom of the press, the right to due process, the right to vote, and equality under the law.

Whether their new experiments with free governments will succeed, only time will tell. They seem, however, to have learned from the American experience that there can be no

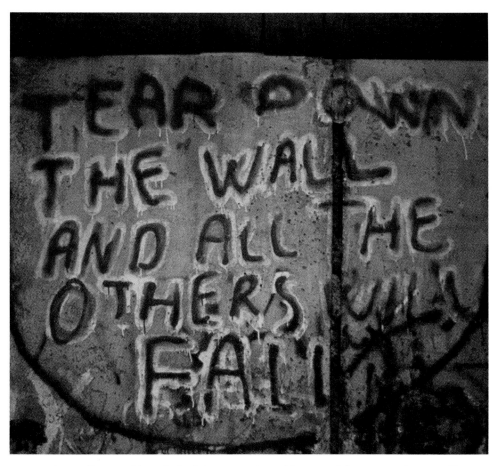

The Berlin Wall, a world symbol of the repression of human rights, came down on Novem-ber 9, 1989. (U.S. Department of Defense)

democracy without a broad commitment to civil rights. Even in the democratic West, the American idea of civil rights inspires imitation. The Canadian Constitution Act of 1982 contained a bill of rights. Even in Britain, in whose experience much of American civil rights are rooted, there has been interest in an American-style bill of rights that would make individual liberties and rights more secure.

There are still many areas of the world where American-style civil rights would be welcomed by many people. The experience of China in 1989, when pro-democracy demonstrations were forcibly and brutally suppressed in Tiananmen Square on June 4, shows that governments still fear the limitations on their power that civil rights provide. The Chinese government provides an example of what life without civil rights is like. After the demonstrations in Tiananmen Square were crushed, the *People's Daily* newspaper proclaimed that the press "must take a clear-cut stand in supporting correct political directions," while the government proceeded to impose censorship and restrict any sort of criticism.

Civil Rights at Home

Even in the United States, Canada, and other nations that have advanced along the path toward full human rights, civil rights will continue to require definition, and controversy will accompany the process as it has in the past. Americans continue to express strong support for the Bill of Rights, but there is little evidence that their understanding of them is increasing. A poll taken by the American Bar Association in the summer of 1991 revealed that only one-third of a random sample of adult Americans could identify the Bill of Rights as the first ten amendments to the Constitution, and only one in ten could correctly identify its original purpose as the protection of individual rights from federal abuse.

The Supreme Court will, as it has in the past, play a key role in settling civil rights controversies. Many believe that appointments to the Court by the Reagan and Bush administrations have given it a much more conservative outlook and that the Court will be less likely than earlier Courts to expand the meaning of civil rights. Some have detected a tendency in the Court to allow more governmental authority over individuals in the form of greater limitation of expression and due process rights, while those who want to preserve the high "wall of separation" between church and state fear that the Court may allow more points of contact between government and religion than in the past. Supporters of the Supreme Court of the 1990's have argued that legislative bodies should have more leeway in making law and that much of the judicial activism of previous decades ought to be reversed — for example, by restricting the rights of those accused of crimes. Past experience, however, indicates that Supreme Court decisions are hard to predict.

A number of areas of future controversy are easy to spot: abortion rights, the relationship between the search and seizure clause and drug testing, affirmative action, the regulation of cable television, and the status of racially offensive speech, to name only a few. The last two are reminders that certain types of situations will require new definitions of rights that, in turn, will provoke controversy.

The relationship of cable television and the First Amendment illustrates the recurring need to adapt constitutional rights to new technology. Cable transmits its signals over wire cables and not over the broadcast spectrum. It thus lacks the technological need of frequency allocation that brought about the government's regulation of broadcasting in the first place. The FCC simply assumed jurisdiction over the cable industry, and in 1984 Congress recognized its authority. The FCC's jurisdiction has been less complete over cable, however, than over broadcast television. Though the Supreme Court has yet to rule on the point, lower federal courts have held that the

FCC cannot regulate content to the same extent as it can with broadcast stations. Another question is the right of local governments to award monopoly franchises to cable companies. Some cable operators have argued that this amounts to government restriction of free expression. The courts will eventually have to decide.

(Mark Reinstein/Uniphoto)

A second type of situation likely to produce future controversy is that in which rights come into conflict. Racially offensive (or "hate") speech is a case in point. Some believe that the Fourteenth Amendment's guarantee of the equal protection of the law should be extended to protect members of minority groups from offensive remarks that are hurtful and psychologically damaging. They argue that such speech should be treated as "fighting words" and is outside First Amendment protection. A number of universities and local governments have sought to limit expression that conveys demeaning and negative racial opinions. Others, even those with little sympathy for racists, argue that there is no constitutional protection against being offended, and that if governments can limit racially biased expression, other limitations on expression will follow. Here, again, the courts will be called upon to decide.

Whenever these contested questions are settled, they are sure to be followed by others. If the past is any predictor of the future, there will be no shortage of different opinions about the meanings of civil rights. This is as it should be. Only by claiming our rights can we maintain them.

Time Line

ca. 2400 B.C. Urukagina, king of Lagash, issues laws to
protect his subjects from having to sell their
property to officials or priests.

ca. 1760 B.C. Hammurabi's Code details the rights of the
Babylonian king's subjects according to social
class.

451-450 B.C. The Laws of the Twelve Tables mark the
beginning of Roman Law, which will recognize
various rights of citizenship.

1215 King John of England agrees to Magna Carta,
foreshadowing the idea of due process.

1606 The Charter of the Virginia Company promises
that colonists will have the rights and liberties
of English subjects.

1628 The Petition of Right is agreed to by England's
Charles I: A king may not imprison without
charge or quarter troops in private homes.

1641 The Massachusetts Body of Liberties is passed.
It provides a list of rights to those accused of
crimes.

1663 The Rhode Island Charter guarantees religious
freedom.

1689 The English Bill of Rights is passed. It prevents
excessive bail and prohibits cruel and unusual
punishments.

1735 John Peter Zenger of the *New York Weekly
Journal* acquitted of seditious libel; truth is
permitted as a defense in such cases.

1776	The Virginia Declaration of Rights is adopted, providing the first constitutional guarantee of individual rights.
1776	The Declaration of Independence is approved, charging England's George III with violating colonists' individual rights.
1788	The U.S. Constitution is ratified.
1791	The Bill of Rights is ratified.
1798	The Sedition Act is passed but fails to silence the opposition press.
1833	In the case *Barron v. Baltimore*, the Supreme Court rules that the Bill of Rights does not apply to the states.
1857	In *Dred Scott v. Sandford*, the Supreme Court rules that blacks, even if free, are not citizens.
1865	The Thirteenth Amendment is ratified, abolishing slavery.
1866	The Civil Rights Act of 1866 passes. It is the first attempt to protect the rights of former slaves.
1868	The Fourteenth Amendment is ratified, requiring "equal protection of the laws."
1870	The Fifteenth Amendment is ratified, protecting black suffrage.
1883	Civil Rights cases are decided by the Supreme Court, limiting the application of the Fourteenth Amendment.
1896	In *Plessy v. Ferguson*, the Supreme Court holds that state-required segregation is legal under the "separate but equal" principle.
1917-1918	Congress passes the Espionage and Sedition Acts, allowing limitations on political expression.
1920	The Nineteenth Amendment is ratified, allowing women to vote in all states.

1925 — In *Gitlow v. New York*, the Supreme Court begins "incorporation" of First Amendment into the Fourteenth Amendment.

1944 — In *Smith v. Allwright*, the Supreme Court rules that all-white primaries are unconstitutional.

1944 — In *Korematsu v. the United States*, the Supreme Court upholds the internment of Japanese Americans.

1954 — In *Brown v. Board of Education of Topeka, Kansas*, the Supreme Court holds that segregated schools are unconstitutional, overturning the "separate but equal" doctrine.

1955 — A bus boycott in Montgomery, Alabama, sets the pattern for nonviolent civil rights demonstrations.

1961 — In *Mapp v. Ohio*, the Supreme Court establishes the "exclusionary rule."

1962 — In *Engel v. Vitale*, the Supreme Court holds that compulsory school prayer is unconstitutional.

1963 — In *Gideon v. Wainwright*, the Supreme Court redefines the Sixth Amendment right to counsel.

1964 — The Twenty-Fourth Amendment ratified, banning poll taxes.

1964 — In *The New York Times v. Sullivan*, the Supreme Court blocks an attempt to use libel law to prevent criticism of public figures.

1964 — The Civil Rights Act of 1964 outlaws racial discrimination in public accommodations.

1965 — In *Griswold v. Connecticut*, the Supreme Court recognizes a constitutional right to privacy.

1965 — The Voting Rights Act of 1965 provides machinery for enforcing the Fifteenth Amendment.

1966	In *Miranda v. Arizona*, the Supreme Court requires that suspects be made aware of their rights upon arrest.
1971	In *The New York Times v. the United States*, the Supreme Court refuses to allow prior censorship of the "Pentagon Papers."
1971	The Twenty-Sixth Amendment is ratified, allowing eighteen-year-olds to vote in all states.
1972	In *Furman v. Georgia*, the Supreme Court temporarily halts capital punishment.
1973	In *Roe v. Wade*, the Supreme Court extends the right of privacy to cover a woman's right to an abortion.
1978	In *Regents of the University of California v. Bakke*, the Supreme Court rules that race may be a factor in admissions procedures but that a rigid quota system is unconstitutional.
1988	In *Hazlewood School District v. Kuhlmeir*, the Supreme Court upholds a school principal's right to edit the content of a school paper.
1989	In *Texas v. Johnson*, the Supreme Court interprets the First Amendment to protect flag-burning as political protest.
1990	In *Employment Division v. Smith*, the Supreme Court upholds the right of Oregon to restrict the use of peyote even if such restriction limits the religious practices of the Native American Church.

Publications

Alderman, Ellen, and Caroline Kennedy. *In Our Defense: The Bill of Rights in Action*. New York: William Morrow, 1991. A book that highlights the relevance of the Bill of Rights to contemporary American life through a series of case studies. Each amendment has at least one chapter that shows a particular right operating in a real-world context. The authors are lawyers writing for a general audience.

Cox, Archibald. *The Court and the Constitution*. Boston: Houghton Mifflin, 1987. One of the best introductions for laypersons to the relationship between the Constitution and the Supreme Court.

Hall, Kermit L., ed. *By and for the People: Constitutional Rights in American History*. Arlington Heights, Ill.: Harlan Davidson, 1991. A very useful volume intended for students and a general audience. Chapters by leading authorities place the major rights in historical context. Excellent reference features include summaries of important cases and bibliographies for each chapter, as well as a glossary.

Hentoff, Nat. *The Day They Came to Arrest the Book*. New York: Dell, 1983. A young-adult novel in which the editor of a school newspaper fights against censorship in the school library.

Irons, Peter. *The Courage of Their Convictions: Sixteen Americans Who Fought Their Way to the Supreme Court*. New York: Free Press, 1988. Accounts of sixteen cases in which individuals claiming rights persisted until reaching the Court. Each chapter includes an account by the author, followed by a first-person account by a participant. One of the latter is Mary Beth Tinker. Irons does a good job of personalizing civil rights for a general audience.

Katz, William Loren, and Bernard Gaughran. *The Constitutional Amendments*. New York: Franklin Watts, 1974. A readable, brief introduction to all twenty-six amendments. One chapter is devoted to each one. A good place for younger readers to start studying the constitutional basis of civil rights.

Klinkner, Philip A., et al. *The American Heritage History of the Bill of Rights*. 10 vols. Englewood Cliffs, N.J.: Silver Burdett Press, 1991. A series for younger readers that devotes one volume to each of the first ten amendments. A good place to begin exploring specific rights.

Kluger, Richard. *Simple Justice: The History of "Brown v. Board of Education" and Black America's Struggle for Equality*. New York: Vintage, 1977. A study of the landmark case that struck down "separate but equal," placing it in the broad context of the African-American experience and carrying its story into the 1960's. Long but readable.

Lewis, Anthony. *Gideon's Trumpet*. New York: Random House, 1964. An account by *The New York Times'* constitutional correspondent of the case that redefined the right to counsel. A readable book that shows how individuals have had an impact on the Constitution.

Morgan, Richard E. *Disabling America: The "Rights Industry" in Our Time*. New York: Basic Books, 1984. A conservative critic argues that the Court has gone too far in recognizing rights, especially new ones, with the result that government is becoming unworkable. Includes a chapter highly critical of the effect of civil rights on law enforcement.

Phillips, Steven. *No Heroes, No Villain: The Story of a Murder*. New York: Random House, 1972. An account of the murder of a New York policeman and subsequent trial. Shows how due process functions in an actual murder case. Accessible to a general audience.

Schwartz, Bernard. *The Great Rights of Mankind: A History of the Bill of Rights*. Expanded edition. Madison, Wisc.: Madison House, 1992. The best historical introduction to the Bill of Rights in an updated edition. Focuses on the origins, birth, and ratification of the Bill of Rights. Concludes with a discussion of recent interpretations.

Taylor, Mildred. *The Friendship*. New York: Dial, 1987. A short young-adult novel set in the days of the Jim Crow laws in the Deep South. Provides insight into life for African Americans before the Civil Rights movement. Winner of the Coretta Scott King Award in 1988.

Uchida, Yoshiko. *Journey to Topaz*. New York: Charles Scribner's Sons, 1971. A young-adult novel about a Japanese-American family that is interned in a Utah camp during World War II.

Media Resources

The Amendments. Film and video, 20 mins. Deerfield, Ill.:
Coronet/MTI, 1987. A brief introduction to the amendment
process, as well as to the twenty-six amendments. For
middle school and older audiences.

Guilty by Reason of Race. Film and video, 57 mins. New York:
National Broadcasting Corporation, 1972. From the NBC
Reports series, a documentary on Japanese-American
relocation during World War II that also examines its
implications for civil rights in general. Interesting
interviews. Middle school and up. Available from many
university film rental services.

Hampton, Henry, executive producer. *Eyes on the Prize, I:
America's Civil Rights Years, 1954-1965*; *Eyes on the Prize,
II: America at the Racial Crossroads, 1965-1985*. Video,
fourteen 60-min. episodes. Boston: Blackside, 1986, 1991.
The best visual account of the modern Civil Rights
movement. Makes effective use of contemporary film clips
and more recent interviews. Available from PBS Video.

Kulish, Mykola, producer and director. *The Road to Brown*.
Video, 47 mins. Charlottesville: University of Virginia,
1990. This documentary traces the background to the
landmark *Brown* decision, stressing the role of Charles H.
Houston, NAACP's chief counsel. Includes interviews with
many participants, including Thurgood Marshall. Available
from California Newsreels.

Moyers, Bill, executive producer. *Moyers: In Search of the
Constitution*. Video, eleven 60-min. episodes. New York:
Public Affairs Television, 1987. One of the best of the

bicentennial series on the Constitution. Covers many topics of interest to students of civil rights, including church-state relations and judicial interpretation. Interviews with several Supreme Court justices. Available from PBS Videos.

Organizations
and
Hotlines

American Bar Association
750 N. Lake Shore Dr.
Chicago, IL 60611
(312) 988-5000
   The major professional organization for lawyers and judges,
the ABA also serves the public by promoting education about
the legal system and law-related issues. A source of
information on the legal and judicial aspects of civil rights.

American Civil Liberties Union
132 W. 43rd St.
New York, NY 10036
(212) 944-9800
   Founded to preserve free speech and rights after World War
I, the ACLU is one of the most forceful advocates of a broad
interpretation of civil rights and liberties. The ACLU often
provides legal assistance when a case raises a significant
rights-related issue. A good source of information for those
seeking a broad interpretation of civil rights.

Association of American Publishers
220 East 23rd St.
New York, NY 10010
(212) 689-8920

The major national organization of commercial publishers. Promotes such positions as copyright protection, freedom to read, and opposition to censorship. A strong advocate of human rights. A good source on First Amendment issues.

League of Women Voters of the United States
1730 M St. NW
Washington, DC 20036
(202) 429-1965
Liberal but nonpartisan group that grew out of the women's suffrage movement. Provides research, publications, and information on political participation. A good source of information on voting rights, registration procedures, government, and other voting matters.

Liberty Federation
2020 Tate Springs Rd.
Lynchburg, VA 24501
(804) 528-5000
Formerly the Moral Majority, the Liberty Federation seeks to promote "family and moral values." Favors constitutional amendments to allow school prayer and ban abortions. Monitors contents of television programming.

Mexican American Legal Defense and Educational Fund
634 Spring St.
Los Angeles, CA 90014
(213) 629-2512
A national organization that focuses on the civil rights of Mexican Americans. Emphasizes such issues as voting rights, immigration law, bilingualism, and discrimination.

National Association for the Advancement of Colored People
4805 Mount Hope Dr.
Baltimore, MD 21215
(212) 481-4100

The oldest, largest, and most influential of civil rights organizations. Primary aim is to promote racial equality. Also opposes capital punishment. A good source on race relations.

National Association of Broadcasters
1771 N St. NW
Washington, DC 20036
(202) 429-5300
A national trade organization of radio and television stations. Offers an extensive list of publications. Has a close relationship with the Federal Communications Commission. A good source on FCC regulation of broadcasting.

National Organization for Women
1401 New York Ave. NW, Suite 800
Washington, DC 20005
(202) 347-2279
Founded in 1966 as the major organization for women's rights. Opposes all forms of discrimination against women and supports passage of an Equal Rights Amendment. A good source on civil rights as they affect women.

National Rifle Association of America
1600 Rhode Island Ave. NW
Washington, DC 20036
(202) 828-6000
Often cited as a model of interest group effectiveness, the NRA seeks to educate the public on the use of firearms. An outspoken and controversial defender of the Second Amendment as an unqualified right to bear arms. Extensive publications. Prime source for information on one side of the gun control issue.

The Newspaper Center
Box 17407

Dulles International Airport
Washington, DC 20041
(703) 648-1000

Formerly the American Newspaper Publishers Association, this is the trade organization of America's daily newspapers. Part of its function is to promote reader education programs. It is particularly interested in First Amendment issues.

Telecommunications Research and Action Center
P.O. Box 12038
Washington, DC 20005
(202) 462-2520

Organized by Ralph Nader as the National Citizens Committee for Broadcasting. Seeks a more democratic and responsive communications system. Publishes newsletters and books to educate the public on media issues and to promote greater public access. Opposes deregulation of broadcasting and favors greater public input on broadcast licensing.

Excerpts from the U.S. Constitution

The Bill of Rights

AMENDMENT 1. Congress shall make no law respecting an establishment of religion, or prohibiting the free exercise thereof; or abridging the freedom of speech, or of the press; or the right of the people peaceably to assemble, and to petition the Government for a redress of grievances.

AMENDMENT 2. A well regulated Militia, being necessary to the security of a free State, the right of the people to keep and bear Arms, shall not be infringed.

AMENDMENT 3. No Soldier shall, in time of peace be quartered in any house, without the consent of the Owner, nor in time of war, but in a manner to be prescribed by law.

AMENDMENT 4. The right of the people to be secure in their persons, houses, papers, and effects, against unreasonable searches and seizures, shall not be violated, and no Warrants shall issue, but upon probable cause, supported by Oath or affirmation, and particularly describing the place to be searched, and the persons or things to be seized.

AMENDMENT 5. No person shall be held to answer for a capital, or otherwise infamous crime, unless on a presentment or indictment of a Grand Jury, except in cases arising in the land or naval forces, or in the Militia, when in actual service in time of War or public danger; nor shall any person be subject for the same offence to be twice put in jeopardy of life or limb; nor shall be compelled in any criminal case to be a witness against himself, nor be deprived of life, liberty, or property, without due process of law; nor shall private property be taken for public use, without just compensation.

AMENDMENT 6. In all criminal prosecutions, the accused shall enjoy the right to a speedy and public trial, by an impartial jury of the State and district wherein the crime shall have been committed, which district shall have been previously ascertained by law, and to be informed of the nature and cause of the accusation; to be confronted with the witnesses against him; to have compulsory process for obtaining witness in his favor, and to have the Assistance of Counsel for his defence.

AMENDMENT 7. In Suits at common law, where the value in controversy shall exceed twenty dollars, the right of trial by jury shall be preserved, and no fact tried by a jury, shall be otherwise re-examined in any Court of the United States, than according to the rules of the common law.

AMENDMENT 8. Excessive bail shall not be required, nor excessive fines imposed, nor cruel and unusual punishments inflicted.

AMENDMENT 9. The enumeration in the Constitution, of certain rights, shall not be construed to deny or disparage others retained by the people.

AMENDMENT 10. The powers not delegated to the United States by the Constitution, nor prohibited by it to the States, are reserved to the States respectively, or to the people.

Other Important Amendments

AMENDMENT 14. *Section 1*. All persons born or naturalized in the United States and subject to the jurisdiction thereof, are citizens of the United States and of the State wherein they reside. No State shall make or enforce any law which shall abridge the privileges or immunities of citizens of the United States; nor shall any State deprive any person of life, liberty, or property, without due process of law; nor deny to any person within its jurisdiction the equal protection of the laws.

AMENDMENT 15. *Section 1.* The right of citizens of the United States to vote shall not be denied or abridged by the United States or by any State on account of race, color, or previous condition of servitude. *Section 2.* The Congress shall have power to enforce this article by appropriate legislation.

AMENDMENT 19. The right of citizens of the United States to vote shall not be denied or abridged by the United States or by any State on account of sex. Congress shall have power to enforce this article by appropriate legislation.

AMENDMENT 24. *Section 1.* The right of citizens of the United States to vote in any primary or other election for President or Vice President, for electors for President or Vice President, or for Senator or Representative in Congress, shall not be denied or abridged by the United States or any State by reason of failure to pay any poll tax or other tax. *Section 2.* The Congress shall have the power to enforce this article by appropriate legislation.

AMENDMENT 26. *Section 1.* The right of citizens of the United States, who are eighteen years of age or older, to vote shall not be denied or abridged by the United States or by any State on account of age. *Section 2.* The Congress shall have the power to enforce this article by appropriate legislation.

INDEX